ALEXANDER POPE

From the portrait by THOMAS HUDSON

P O P E

Poetry & Prose

With Essays by

JOHNSON, COLERIDGE, HAZLITT

&c.

With an Introduction and Notes by

H. V. D. DYSON

OXFORD
AT THE CLARENDON PRESS

Oxford University Press, Amen House, London E.C.4

GLASGOW NEW YORK TORONTO MELBOURNE WELLINGTON

BOMBAY CALCUTTA MADRAS KARACHI LAHORE DACCA

CAPE TOWN SALISBURY NAIROBI IBADAN ACCRA

KUALA LUMPUR HONG KONG

FIRST PUBLISHED 1933

REPRINTED 1939, 1941, 1942, 1946, 1947

1949, 1951, 1953, 1961, 1964

PRINTED IN GREAT BRITAIN

CONTENTS

INTRODUCTION

Pope's earliest poems show conventionality in subject and outlook, but freshness and vigour of execution. The thought in so far as it is separable from the poetry is usually commonplace. 'Like gentle Fanny's was his flowering theme, a painted mistress, or a purling stream.' The first collected edition of his Works (1717) contains little of the eloquent indignation which was to give colour and movement to so much of his later writing, and reveals more capacity for graceful compliment than for trenchant satire. Beyond a casual flick at Appius in *An Essay on Criticism* and Sir Plume in *The Rape of the Lock*, his criticisms are general and inoffensive. The elaborate reproof meted out to 'the false guardian of a charge too good' in the *Elegy to the Memory of an Unfortunate Lady* is of perishable stuff and no individual could have resented it. Keen observation of details, with just a hint of contemptuous invective kept well in reserve, perhaps suggests the future 'dreaded satirist', but there is as yet no touch of real bitterness. Moreover, in his preface to this volume he puts forward a remarkable plea on behalf of those whom his changed and matured genius was later to consign to *The Dunciad*.

'I think a good deal may be said to extenuate the fault of bad Poets. What we call a Genius, is hard to be distinguish'd by a man himself, from a strong inclination: and if it be never so great, he can not at first discover it any other way, than by that prevalent propensity which renders him the more liable to be mistaken. The only method he has, is to make the experiment by writing, and appealing to the judgment of others: And if he happens to write ill (which is certainly no sin in itself) he is immediately made an object of ridicule. I wish we had the humanity to reflect that even the worst authors might endeavour to please us, and in that endeavour, deserve something at our hands. We have no cause to quarrel with them but for their obstinacy in persisting, and this too may admit of alleviating circumstances. Their particular friends may be either ignorant, or insincere; and the rest of the world too well bred to shock them with a truth, which generally their Booksellers are the first that inform them of. This happens not till they have spent too much of their time, to apply to any profession which might better fit their talents; and till such talents as they have are so far discredited, as to be but of small service to them. For (what is the hardest case imaginable) the reputation of a man generally depends upon the first steps he makes in the world, and people will establish their opinion of us, from what we do at that season when we have least judgment to direct us.'

Pope's own first steps had been supremely fortunate, and at the time he wrote this he was already a famous poet whose acquaintance was eagerly sought. Although he had not yet 'stoop'd to Truth and moraliz'd his song', this collected edition, printed when he was twenty-nine, contains some of his best poems and affords ample evidence of the range and variety of his interests.

The *Pastorals*, though thin, show not infrequently new and subtle melodies enriching an unconvincing diction. *An Essay on Criticism* testifies to his serious interest in poetry and its problems. While it adds nothing of value to critical theory, it remains a brilliant specimen of a literary fashion which had hitherto failed to rise above a pedestrian level. *Windsor Forest*, a beautiful poem which gives him a place among our descriptive poets and shows the measure of his sensitiveness to natural beauty, shows also how little Nature had to do with the development of his 'moral being'. *The Rape of the Lock*, the best Society poem ever written, reveals a delighted, almost girlish attraction to the vanities and foibles of a 'smart set' and an equal pleasure in malicious and witty comment on such trifles. Its theme stimulated his imagination as nothing hitherto had done, and the delicate pattern of its structure and the varied gleams and swift, clear music of its verse reflect not only the artist's joy in the thing he is making but also the observer's pleasure in the graceful futilities he is contemplating. Its beauty is that of delight made visible; a sophisticated malice-flecked delight to which even those who as a rule do not care for Pope are glad to surrender. Pope's instinctive interest in the feminine world reminds us of his association with Steele and Addison. *The Rape of the Lock* has something of the touch of cynical patronage with which *The Spectator* treated the fair sex; but his own characteristic note of sentiment is perhaps seen most clearly in the playful tenderness of *On a Young Lady's leaving Town after the Coronation.* This side of his nature is often forgotten. Dependent as he was on the assistance of women in the daily details of his semi-invalid existence, he was eager too for their intellectual companionship and appreciation. His long friendship with Martha Blount and the pleasure he took in being associated with Lady Mary Wortley Montagu show this. He quarrelled bitterly with Lady Mary in later years, but for a long time he valued her friendship highly and she seems in some degree to have inspired *Eloisa to Abelard.* He was always ready to enter into archly intimate correspondence with young women like Judith Cowper, ready also with his officious partisanship in affairs like that which is commemorated in the *Elegy,* and he thoroughly enjoyed interfering in the Fermor-Petre squabble. The kindness of his women friends, which survived the absurdly gallant tone in which he sometimes wrote to them, allowed him to forget the freakish body which set him so far apart from ordinary men.

His first official appearance as an etcher of satiric portraits was in March, 1728, two months before the publication of *The Dunciad,* when he included in the third volume of his and Swift's *Miscellanies* (dated 1727) the *Fragment of a Satire* which, with slight changes, was later worked into the *Epistle to Arbuthnot* (ll. 151–214). This seems to have been his first acknowledgement of the 'character of Addison', which had been long understood to be his. He had, however, given earlier proof of a vigorous spirit of retaliation, though only once did he produce anything at all memorable. On April 27, 1713, there was published a number of *The Guardian* (No. 40) in which the excessive praise that Addison's 'little senate' at Button's coffee-house had lavished on Ambrose Philips's *Pastorals* was travestied in a vein of cool irony. Pope's own *Pastorals* had for some years, while still in manuscript, been applauded by such wits as Walsh and Granville, and when at last they were printed in Tonson's *Sixth Miscellany* (1709) Philips's appeared in the same volume. Pope could not fail to mark the surprising enthusiasm with which Addison's circle greeted his rival's work. With this paper he declared himself independent of that group, and later in the same year he became intimate with Swift, the chief man of letters of the Tories, the course of whose friendship with Addison had been checked by politics. Pope and Swift, with Arbuthnot and Gay and Parnell, formed the Scriblerus Club.

Pope seems originally to have intended *The Dunciad* to appear in the above-mentioned volume of *Miscellanies*, after being printed first as a separate piece. Writing to Benjamin Motte, his publisher, on June 30, 1727, he says: 'As to the poem which I will have to end the volume, it will make three sheets at least, and I will take time till winter to finish it. It may then be published, singly first if proper. I'm sure it will be advantageous so to do—but say not a word of it to any man.' But either the poem swelled to unmanageable proportions or he was unable to finish it in time, for the book appeared without it and instead at the beginning was the essay *On the Art of Sinking in Poetry,* which had been destined for a subsequent volume of prose *Miscellanies.* This essay, with its personal and provocative sixth chapter, drew a good deal of answering fire, and so, designedly or not, *The Dunciad* had something of the appearance of a counter-attack.

The survivors of the Scriblerus group were assembled once more and the long-maturing fruits of that old companionship of 1713–14 came to ripeness within a period of eighteen months. *Gulliver's Travels* appeared in October 1726, *The Beggar's Opera* in January 1728, *The Dunciad* in May of the same year. The *Dunciad* is Pope's greatest poem. In a sense it is his only 'great' original poem. Great in the disciplined assault of its powerful verse, great in intensity, it is greatest of all in its power of appealing successfully to our imagination against the indictments which our modern taste not infrequently frames against it. Pope consistently assumes that Poverty is the result of bad writing, and a kindlier age replies that bad writing is sufficiently avenged. But the Poverty which Pope ridiculed was not simple misery; it was a Poverty strident, eloquent, and, so it must have appeared to him, actively malignant. From the Grub Street section of the writing world had come some of his most persistent assailants. Moreover, he had only freed himself from the fear of personal poverty by twelve years of hard, often uncongenial, work. Both these points are important. 'Certain laws by sufferers thought unjust' were an abiding threat to the prosperity of English Roman Catholics. They paid double taxes and usually found it expedient to invest their money in foreign securities which their own country's triumphs did nothing to appreciate. Alexander Pope senior was not a rich man, and from time to time he and his family were unpleasantly reminded of the disabilities under which they and their co-religionists suffered. So his son translated

Homer and attained the freedom and security which a small fortune confers. In his *Imitation of Horace,* Epistle 2, Book II, he tells us:

> For Right Hereditary tax'd and fin'd,
> He[1] stuck to poverty with peace of mind;
> And me the Muses help'd to undergo it;
> Convict a Papist he, and I a Poet.
> But (thanks to Homer) since I live and thrive,
> Indebted to no Prince or Peer alive.

Pope as a semi-invalid required the attendance and comforts that only money could give. Also he was, like most good poets of the time, a Society poet. It was not so much that he found the motives and subjects of his poems among the interests of the cultured few, as that he needed the friendship and company of good minds. He could neither live nor work alone, and he had won the right to share the life of the educated members of the ruling class. His religion shut him out from the professions, and from posts under the Government such as from time to time were enjoyed by Congreve, Prior, Addison, and Steele. It would have been easy for him to have followed Gay's example and lived on patronage. But such a course he despised, and there is no conclusive evidence that he ever received a present of money from any of his friends.

His *Homer* is epic in a double sense. It represents the most heroic effort of will he ever made. He secured immunity alike from 'the patron and the jail' but at the cost of serious inroads on his limited supply of nervous energy. There is something fragmentary or piecemeal about all his subsequent work. He completed only portions of his projected great moral poem, and even at *The Dunciad,* his 'minor epic', his nearest approach to an original poem on the grand scale, he patched and tinkered for years. His

[1] The elder Pope.

friends realized his difficulties. Swift writing to him on July 19, 1725, says:

'Our Lord Oxford[1] used to curse the occasions that put you on translations, and, if he and the Queen had lived, you should have entirely followed your own genius, built and planted much, and writ only when you had a mind.'

A little earlier with reference to the *Odyssey* he had written to Lord Oxford,[2] November 27, 1724:

'I doubt Mr. Pope's voyage into Homer-land will bring more profit than reputation, and I wish his fortunes could afford him to employ his own genius. I have been told this voyage is to supply what he lost by a former into the South Sea.'

From 1711 onwards, all the time he was consolidating his reputation and laboriously building up his small fortune, he had been persistently subjected, by men who were themselves failures or insignificant, to abuse in pamphlet and lampoon. Some ridiculed his person, some contemned his abilities, some decried his morals. About 1726, the year of Swift's first visit since his exile in Ireland, Pope's position was in many ways less strong than it had been. His translation of the *Iliad* (finished 1720) had been acknowledged to be a brilliant success, although scholars like Bentley (Aristarchus in *The Dunciad*) might sneer, but many readers were dissatisfied with the *Odyssey* (finished 1726). His edition of his old friend the Duke of Buckingham's *Works* (1723) had excited the suspicion of the Government on account of its Jacobite tendencies. His *Shakespeare* (1725) had not even brought him much profit and had exposed him to the telling criticism of Lewis Theobald, who, although he had none of Pope's genius was better qualified as an editor and textual critic. It was to *Shakespeare Restor'd* (1726) that Theobald owed, though he did not deserve, his place as King of the Dunces

[1] Robert, 1st Earl of Oxford and Mortimer, *ob*. May, 1714.
[2] Edward, 2nd Earl.

in the earlier version of *The Dunciad.* Pope was hard put to it to find a hero, and circumstances crowned the most reasonable of his critics.

We ought therefore to remember that when Pope attacks Poverty he is bitterly mindful of the exertions he had made to escape from it, and, proud of his own success, is contemptuous and hard towards those who for long years had hindered him. It must have seemed intolerable that he should continue to afford sport to dull writers and continue also to endure without reply the criticism of men like Bentley and Theobald, whom with some justification he had grown to regard as pedantic enemies of imaginative writing. But it is only just also to remember that some of the victims of *The Art of Sinking* and *The Dunciad* are not known to have offered provocation, a fact of which they took full advantage in their replies. The claims of human charity to which he, the friend of Thomson and benefactor of Savage, responded so liberally in his private life, found small place in his satire. But in *The Dunciad* we have more than the mere slaughter of Pope's enemies. We feel also that he is defending and vindicating something that he values. He has in fact built a citadel for the defence of the ideals of Augustan culture, a culture which was not democratic although it recruited widely. Talent no less than birth and wealth could find a place within its narrow circle and good writers whatever their origin were made welcome. But its ideals, implicitly defended in *The Dunciad,* were definitely aristocratic, the ideals of leisured good breeding. And so we have the last completely undemocratic poem in English. But Grub Street was not wholly inhabited by dunces. In May 1738 Samuel Johnson's *London* was published simultaneously with one of the last of Pope's Horatian poems. Grub Street had provided an answer, whose quality Pope was quick to appreciate and applaud.

The lack of narrative unity detracts little from the interest of *The Dunciad*. Pope had not the dramatic instinct that can make myths, but the world of triumphant Dulness progressively revealed has a unity of its own, and the shaping power of his angry intuition makes the poem a whole despite its digressions and revisions. What he was looking at did not alter, and its menace was, and is, a real one. In the First Book, which can be read as a separate and complete poem, are exhibited to the full the variety and vivacity of his satiric powers, and the famous passage which closes the whole, a movement matchless in music and dark splendour, remains unstaled by praise.

The Essay on Man, though to-day better known, is far less successful. The truth is that Pope neither knew enough nor felt enough about its subject. There are many memorable passages and the language is always alive, but the poem as a whole lacks the conviction and drive of *The Dunciad*. The easy good breeding of the world in which he lived did not make for deeply held convictions.

> But ask not, to what Doctors I apply?[1]
> Sworn to no Master, of no Sect am I:
> As drives the storm, at any door I knock:
> And house with Montaigne now, or now with Locke.
> Sometimes a Patriot, active in debate,
> Mix with the World, and battle for the State,
> Free as young Lyttelton, her cause pursue,
> Still true to Virtue, and as warm as true:
> Sometimes with Aristippus, or St. Paul,
> Indulge my Candor, and grow all to all;
> Back to my native Moderation slide,
> And win my way by yielding to the tide.

It is true that his personal friendships tended to harden his political attitude during the last fifteen years or so of his life, when he became increasingly the Laureate of the

[1] *Imitations of Horace*, Epistle 1, Bk. 1, ll. 23–34.

'Patriotic' opposition to Walpole. Times were changing and Walpole was developing a new political technique. He valued steady support of his own government above the persuasive charms of wit and literature. No one ever played Swift to his Harley. Although his personal relations with Pope were not unfriendly, he looked with natural suspicion on the survivors of the Scriblerus group with their high Tory tradition. Above all he was resolved never to trust Bolingbroke, who, after his return to England in 1723 until his final return to exile, was perhaps Pope's chief friend. During these later years Pope was a figure somewhat less fully representative of the entire ruling class, and was 'content with the praise of half the nation'. But this political impulse, clearly marked in the *Epistle to Augustus* and in the *Epilogue to the Satires*, robbed his poetry of nothing of its power.

Pope was in many ways a spoiled child of genius and the world into which he made his way by his rare gifts was content to accept him in the only way one can accept a spoiled child—on his own terms. Born of elderly parents whose care he repaid with deep affection, he was extremely precocious and apparently equally attractive. In his youth he fascinated the established wits and poets of the Town as well as the country gentlemen of Berkshire, his father's neighbours: in his maturity he was courted and followed by younger men like Orrery, Marchmont, and Lyttelton. Men whom living we should most have wished to meet, whose acquaintance we should most have coveted, were proud to be his friends. He quarrelled with only one man of first-rate ability, if indeed the wretched misunderstandings with Addison can be dignified by the name of quarrels. For Addison, totally incompatible as was his character with Pope's, was not the man to enjoy a feud. Dislike he might, distrust he did the much younger wit who disturbed the serenity of Button's, but he avoided an open breach.

Many of Pope's least lovable characteristics were due to his physical disabilities. He was a dwarf, almost indeed a cripple, with a cripple's acute sensitiveness, and needed all the encouragement and praise which were lavished on him. Influenced very much by stronger characters, he took colour readily from his intellectual environment, and no poet has more completely identified himself with the tastes and opinions of his age. He was as quick to adopt fashionable behaviour as fashionable thought, quick also to make his own the prejudices and intolerances of his circle. He found a place in the last really stable and civilized society this country has seen—a society which, although it produced no poetry of the very highest kind, cared much for poetry and whose favourite poet he was.

Pope deliberately took his place in the English poetic tradition, which he upheld and developed. He shared the current view that poetry was a great instrument of moral improvement and that its most effective method was that of satire, which by its ridicule destroyed corrupt customs and exposed the wicked. In him the quickly kindled anger of the satirist combined with an exceptionally delicate poetic sensibility. To appreciate his poetry requires both experience and intelligence. We may miss in it the freedom we are accustomed to associate with the work of the great poets of the nineteenth century. It has about it no vague nobility, no enchantment. Pope wholesomely reminds us of those fantastic tricks that, dressed in a little brief authority, we play before high Heaven. In a sense we are all his victims. Satire is less free than other forms of poetry because of its necessarily close and immediate relation to the world of everyday habit and experience. Its objects must always be recognizable whether they are persons or vices. Satire tells the truth, but for its own high purpose emphasizes those aspects of the truth that are discreditable. It gives us knowledge, as does all poetry, of the permanent structure of our minds and strengthens us by the revelation of man's power to chastise his own weaknesses. So Pope triumphed over his disabilities, religious, social, and personal. He lived to become a name of power and to see 'men not afraid of God, afraid of *him*'. He relieved the finest of English satires by the most perfect of English courtly compliments. Utterly unrebellious, he held that good was preferable to evil, and that good and evil themselves were what three thousand years of experience had shown them to be.

POPE'S LIFE

1688. Alexander Pope born in London, 21 May, the only child of elderly parents.

1700. Pope's family moved to Binfield, near Wokingham, Berkshire, where they lived till 1716.

1709. *Pastorals* published in Jacob Tonson's Miscellany, vol. vi. The volume contained also his *January and May*, and the Pastorals of Ambrose Philips.

1711. (May) *An Essay on Criticism.*
Pope comes to know Gay, Steele, and Addison.

1712. (May) *The Rape of the Lock* (in two cantos) published in Bernard Lintot's Miscellany, with other poems by Pope. *Messiah* published in *The Spectator*, No. 378 (14 May).

1713. (March) *Windsor Forest*; Prologue to Addison's *Cato* (acted 14 April); *Ode on St. Cecilia's Day*; Essays in *The Guardian.*
Pope comes to know Swift. Subscriptions for *Homer* opened. Meetings of the Scriblerus Club (1713–14).

1714. (March) *The Rape of the Lock,* enlarged to five cantos.
Queen Anne died 4 August.

1715. (February) *The Temple of Fame.*
(6 June) *The Iliad,* vol. i, Books i–iv.

1716. *The Iliad,* vol. ii, Books v–viii.
Pope's family moved to Mawson's Buildings, Chiswick.

1717. (June) *The Works of Mr. Alexander Pope,* including *Verses to the Memory of an Unfortunate Lady* and *Eloisa to Abelard.*
(June) *The Iliad,* vol. iii, Books ix–xii.
Death of Pope's father, 23 October.

1718. *The Iliad,* vol. iv, Books xiii–xvi.

1719. Pope moved with his mother to Twickenham.

1720. (May) *The Iliad,* vols. v and vi, Books xvii–xxiv.
The South Sea Bubble.

1721. 'Epistle to Addison' (*Moral Essays,* v) published in Tickell's edition of Addison's *Works*; 'Epistle to Robert Earl of Oxford' published in Pope's edition of Parnell's *Poems* (dated 1722).

1722. 'Character of Atticus' printed without Pope's authority in *The St. James's Journal,* 15 December.

1723. *The Works of John Sheffield, Duke of Buckingham,* edited by Pope.

1725. (March) *The Works of Shakespear,* in six volumes, edited by Pope.
(April) *The Odyssey,* vols. i–iii, Books i–xiv.

1726. *The Odyssey*, vols. iv and v, Books xv–xxiv.
Swift visits Pope (*Gulliver's Travels* published 28 October).

1727. *Miscellanies*, vols. i and ii, by Pope and Swift.
Second visit of Swift.

1728. (March) *Miscellanies*, vol. iii (containing 'Peri Bathous: of the Art of Sinking in Poetry').
(May) *The Dunciad* (three books, with Theobald as hero).

1729. 'Variorum' edition of *The Dunciad*.

1731–5. *Moral Essays*, i–iv: Of the Use of Riches (to Lord Burlington), December 1731; Of the Use of Riches (to Lord Bathurst), January 1733; Of the Knowledge and Characters of Men (to Lord Cobham), January 1734; Of the Characters of Women, February 1735.

1733–4. *An Essay on Man*, Epistles I–III, February–May 1733; Epistle IV, January 1734.

1733–8. *Satires and Epistles of Horace Imitated*: First Satire of the Second Book of Horace (to Mr. Fortescue), February 1733; Second Satire of the Second Book of Horace (to Mr. Bethel), July 1734; First Epistle of the Second Book of Horace (to Augustus), May 1737; Second Epistle of the Second Book of Horace (to Colonel Cotterell), April 1737; Sixth Epistle of the First Book of Horace (to Mr. Murray), January 1738; First Epistle of the First Book of Horace (to Lord Bolingbroke), March 1738, but dated 1737.

1733. Pope's mother died, 7 June.

1735. (January) *Epistle to Arbuthnot*.
(April) *The Works of Mr. Alexander Pope*, vol. ii (containing Poems subsequent to 1717).
(May) *Mr. Pope's Literary Correspondence*, printed for Curll.

1737. (May) *Letters of Mr. Alexander Pope*—authorized edition.

1738. The Rev. William Warburton, afterwards Bishop of Gloucester, begins to defend the *Essay on Man* against the criticisms of Jean Pierre de Crousaz; meets Pope in 1740.
One Thousand Seven Hundred and Thirty-Eight, Dialogue I, May; Dialogue II, July—afterwards called *Epilogue to the Satires*.
(June) *The Universal Prayer*.

1740. *Selecta Poemata Italorum* edited by Pope.

1741. *The Works of Mr. Alexander Pope, in Prose*, vol. ii, containing the *Memoirs of Scriblerus*.

1742. (March) *The New Dunciad: As it was found in the Year 1741*, called 'Book the Fourth'.

1743. (October) *The Dunciad, in Four Books*, with Cibber as hero.

1744. Pope dies of dropsy and asthma at Twickenham, 30 May.

From JOHNSON'S

Life of Pope

1781

OF his intellectual character the constituent and fundamental principle was Good Sense, a prompt and intuitive perception of consonance and propriety. He saw immediately, of his own conceptions, what was to be chosen, and what to be rejected; and in the works of others, what was to be shunned, and what was to be copied.

But good sense alone is a sedate and quiescent quality, which manages its possessions well, but does not increase them; it collects few materials for its own operations, and preserves safety, but never gains supremacy. Pope had likewise genius; a mind active, ambitious, and adventurous, always investigating, always aspiring; in its widest searches still longing to go forward, in its highest flights still wishing to be higher; always imagining something greater than it knows, always endeavouring more than it can do.

To assist these powers he is said to have had great strength and exactness of memory. That which he had heard or read was not easily lost; and he had before him not only what his own meditation suggested, but what he had found in other writers that might be accommodated to his present purpose.

These benefits of nature he improved by incessant and unwearied diligence; he had recourse to every source of intelligence, and lost no opportunity of information; he consulted the living as well as the dead; he read his compositions to his friends, and was never content with mediocrity when excellence could be attained. He considered poetry as the business of his life, and, however he might seem to lament his occupation, he followed it with constancy; to make verses was his first labour, and to mend them was his last.

From his attention to poetry he was never diverted. If conversation offered any thing that could be improved, he committed it to paper; if a thought, or perhaps an expression more happy than was common, rose to his mind, he was careful to write it; an independent distich was preserved for an opportunity of insertion, and some little fragments have been found containing lines, or parts of lines, to be wrought upon at some other time.

He was one of those few whose labour is their pleasure: he was never elevated to negligence, nor wearied to impatience; he never passed a fault unamended by indifference, nor quitted it by despair. He laboured his works first to gain reputation, and afterwards to keep it.

Of composition there are different methods. Some employ at once memory and invention, and, with little intermediate use of the pen, form and polish large masses by continued meditation, and write their productions only when, in their own opinion, they have completed them. It is related of Virgil that his custom was to pour out a great number of verses in the morning, and pass the day in retrenching exuberances and correcting inaccuracies. The method of Pope, as may be collected from his translation, was to write his first thoughts in his first words, and gradually to amplify, decorate, rectify, and refine them.

With such faculties and such dispositions he excelled every other writer in *poetical prudence*; he wrote in such a manner as might expose him to few hazards. He used almost always the same fabric of verse; and, indeed, by those few essays which he made of any other, he did not enlarge his reputation. Of this uniformity the certain consequence was readiness and dexterity. By perpetual practice language had in his mind a systematical arrangement;

having always the same use for words, he had words so selected and combined as to be ready at his call. This increase of facility he confessed himself to have perceived in the progress of his translation.

But what was yet of more importance, his effusions were always voluntary, and his subjects chosen by himself. His independence secured him from drudging at a task, and labouring upon a barren topic: he never exchanged praise for money, nor opened a shop of condolence or congratulation. His poems, therefore, were scarce ever temporary. He suffered coronations and royal marriages to pass without a song, and derived no opportunities from recent events, nor any popularity from the accidental disposition of his readers. He was never reduced to the necessity of soliciting the sun to shine upon a birthday, of calling the Graces and Virtues to a wedding, or of saying what multitudes have said before him. When he could produce nothing new, he was at liberty to be silent.

His publications were for the same reason never hasty. He is said to have sent nothing to the press till it had lain two years under his inspection: it is at least certain that he ventured nothing without nice examination. He suffered the tumult of imagination to subside, and the novelties of invention to grow familiar. He knew that the mind is always enamoured of its own productions, and did not trust his first fondness. He consulted his friends, and listened with great willingness to criticism; and, what was of more importance, he consulted himself, and let nothing pass against his own judgement.

He professed to have learned his poetry from Dryden, whom, whenever an opportunity was presented, he praised through his whole life with unvaried liberality; and perhaps his character may receive some illustration if he be compared with his master.

Integrity of understanding and nicety of discernment were not allotted in a less proportion to Dryden than to Pope. The rectitude of Dryden's mind was sufficiently shown by the dismission of his poetical prejudices, and the rejection of unnatural thoughts and rugged numbers. But Dryden never desired to apply all the judgement that he had. He wrote, and professed to write, merely for the people; and when he pleased others, he contented himself. He spent no time in struggles to rouse latent powers; he never attempted to make that better which was already good, nor often to mend what he must have known to be faulty. He wrote, as he tells us, with very little consideration; when occasion or necessity called upon him, he poured out what the present moment happened to supply, and, when once it had passed the press, ejected it from his mind; for when he had no pecuniary interest, he had no further solicitude.

Pope was not content to satisfy; he desired to excel, and therefore always endeavoured to do his best: he did not court the candour, but dared the judgement of his reader, and, expecting no indulgence from others, he showed none to himself. He examined lines and words with minute and punctilious observation, and retouched every part with indefatigable diligence, till he had left nothing to be forgiven.

For this reason he kept his pieces very long in his hands, while he considered and reconsidered them. The only poems which can be supposed to have been written with such regard to the times as might hasten their publication, were the two satires of *Thirty-eight*; of which Dodsley told me that they were brought to him by the author, that they might be fairly copied. 'Almost every line', he said, 'was then written twice over; I gave him a clean transcript, which he sent some time afterwards to me for the press, with almost every line written twice over a second time.'

His declaration that his care for his works ceased at their

publication was not strictly true. His parental attention never abandoned them; what he found amiss in the first edition, he silently corrected in those that followed. He appears to have revised the *Iliad*, and freed it from some of its imperfections; and the *Essay on Criticism* received many improvements after its first appearance. It will seldom be found that he altered without adding clearness, elegance, or vigour. Pope had perhaps the judgement of Dryden; but Dryden certainly wanted the diligence of Pope.

In acquired knowledge the superiority must be allowed to Dryden, whose education was more scholastic, and who before he became an author had been allowed more time for study, with better means of information. His mind has a larger range, and he collects his images and illustrations from a more extensive circumference of science. Dryden knew more of man in his general nature, and Pope in his local manners. The notions of Dryden were formed by comprehensive speculation, and those of Pope by minute attention. There is more dignity in the knowledge of Dryden, and more certainty in that of Pope.

Poetry was not the sole praise of either, for both excelled likewise in prose; but Pope did not borrow his prose from his predecessor. The style of Dryden is capricious and varied, that of Pope is cautious and uniform; Dryden obeys the motions of his own mind, Pope constrains his mind to his own rules of composition. Dryden is sometimes vehement and rapid; Pope is always smooth, uniform, and gentle. Dryden's page is a natural field, rising into inequalities, and diversified by the varied exuberance of abundant vegetation; Pope's is a velvet lawn, shaven by the scythe, and levelled by the roller.

Of genius, that power which constitutes a poet; that quality without which judgement is cold and knowledge is inert; that energy which collects, combines, amplifies, and animates; the superiority must, with some hesitation, be allowed to Dryden. It is not to be inferred that of this poetical vigour Pope had only a little, because Dryden had more, for every other writer since Milton must give place to Pope; and even of Dryden it must be said that if he has brighter paragraphs, he has not better poems. Dryden's performances were always hasty, either excited by some external occasion, or extorted by domestic necessity; he composed without consideration, and published without correction. What his mind could supply at call, or gather in one excursion, was all that he sought, and all that he gave. The dilatory caution of Pope enabled him to condense his sentiments, to multiply his images, and to accumulate all that study might produce, or chance might supply. If the flights of Dryden therefore are higher, Pope continues longer on the wing. If of Dryden's fire the blaze is brighter, of Pope's the heat is more regular and constant. Dryden often surpasses expectation, and Pope never falls below it. Dryden is read with frequent astonishment, and Pope with perpetual delight.

This parallel will, I hope, when it is well considered, be found just; and if the reader should suspect me, as I suspect myself, of some partial fondness for the memory of Dryden, let him not too hastily condemn me; for meditation and inquiry may, perhaps, show him the reasonableness of my determination. . . .

One of his greatest though of his earliest works is the *Essay on Criticism*, which if he had written nothing else would have placed him among the first critics and the first poets, as it exhibits every mode of excellence that can embellish or dignify didactic composition, selection of matter, novelty of arrangement, justness of precept, splendour of illustration, and propriety of digression. I know not whether it be pleasing to consider that he produced this piece at twenty, and never afterwards excelled it: he that delights himself with observing that such powers may be so soon attained, cannot but grieve to think that life was ever after at a stand.

To mention the particular beauties of the *Essay* would be unprofitably tedious; but I cannot forbear to observe that the comparison of a student's progress in the sciences with the journey of a traveller in the Alps is perhaps the best that English poetry can show. A simile, to be perfect, must both illustrate and ennoble the subject; must show it to the understanding in a clearer view, and display it to the fancy with greater dignity: but either of these qualities may be sufficient to recommend it. In didactic poetry, of which the great purpose is instruction, a simile may be praised which illustrates, though it does not ennoble; in heroics, that may be admitted which ennobles, though it does not illustrate. That it may be complete it is required to exhibit, independently of its references, a pleasing image; for a simile is said to be a short episode. To this antiquity was so attentive that circumstances were sometimes added, which, having no parallels, served only to fill the imagination, and produced what Perrault ludicrously called 'comparisons with a long tail'. In their similes the greatest writers have sometimes failed: the ship-race, compared with the chariot-race, is neither illustrated nor aggrandized; land and water make all the difference: when Apollo running after Daphne is likened to a greyhound chasing a hare, there is nothing gained; the ideas of pursuit and flight are too plain to be made plainer, and a god and the daughter of a god are not represented much to their advantage by a hare and dog. The simile of the Alps has no useless parts, yet affords a striking picture by itself: it makes the foregoing position better understood, and enables it to take faster hold on the attention; it assists the apprehension, and elevates the fancy. . . .

To the praises which have been accumulated on *The Rape of the Lock* by readers of every class, from the critic to the waiting-maid, it is difficult to make any addition. Of that which is universally allowed to be the most attractive of all ludicrous compositions, let it rather be now inquired from what sources the power of pleasing is derived.

Dr. Warburton, who excelled in critical perspicacity, has remarked that the preternatural agents are very happily adapted to the purposes of the poem. The heathen deities can no longer gain attention: we should have turned away from a contest between Venus and Diana. The employment of allegorical persons always excites conviction of its own absurdity: they may produce effects, but cannot conduct actions; when the phantom is put in motion, it dissolves; thus Discord may raise a mutiny, but Discord cannot conduct a march, nor besiege a town. Pope brought into view a new race of Beings, with powers and passions proportionate to their operation. The sylphs and gnomes act at the toilet and the tea-table, what more terrific and more powerful phantoms perform on the stormy ocean or the field of battle; they give their proper help, and do their proper mischief.

Pope is said by an objector not to have been the inventor of this petty nation; a charge which might with more justice have been brought against the author of the *Iliad*, who doubtless adopted the religious system of his country; for what is there but the names of his agents which Pope has not invented? Has he not assigned them characters and operations never heard of before? Has he not, at least, given them their first poetical existence? If this is not sufficient to denominate his work original, nothing original ever can be written.

In this work are exhibited in a very high degree the two most engaging powers of an author. New things are made familiar, and familiar things are made new. A race of aerial people never heard of before is presented to us in a manner so clear and easy, that the reader seeks for no further information, but immediately mingles with his new acquaintance, adopts their interests and attends their pursuits, loves a sylph and detests a gnome.

That familiar things are made new, every paragraph will prove. The subject of the poem is an event below the common incidents of common life; nothing real is introduced that is not seen so often as to be no longer regarded, yet the whole detail of a female-day is here brought before us invested with so much art of decoration that, though nothing is disguised, every thing is striking, and we feel all the appetite of curiosity for that from which we have a thousand times turned fastidiously away. . . .

The Epistle of *Eloise to Abelard* is one of the most happy productions of human wit: the subject is so judiciously chosen that it would be difficult, in turning over the annals of the world, to find another which so many circumstances concur to recommend. We regularly interest ourselves most in the fortune of those who most deserve our notice. Abelard and Eloise were conspicuous in their days for eminence of merit. The heart naturally loves truth. The adventures and misfortunes of this illustrious pair are known from undisputed history. Their fate does not leave the mind in hopeless dejection; for they both found quiet and consolation in retirement and piety. So new and so affecting is their story that it supersedes invention, and imagination ranges at full liberty without straggling into scenes of fable.

The story thus skilfully adopted has been diligently improved. Pope has left nothing behind him which seems more the effect of studious perseverance and laborious revisal.

Here is particularly observable the *curiosa felicitas*, a fruitful soil, and careful cultivation. Here is no crudeness of sense, nor asperity of language. . . .

The train of my disquisition has now conducted me to that poetical wonder, the translation of the *Iliad*; a performance which no age or nation can pretend to equal. . . . The chief help of Pope in this arduous undertaking was drawn from the versions of Dryden. Virgil had borrowed much of his imagery from Homer, and part of the debt was now paid by his translator. Pope searched the pages of Dryden for happy combinations of heroic diction; but it will not be denied that he added much to what he found. He cultivated our language with so much diligence and art that he has left in his *Homer* a treasure of poetical elegances to posterity. His version may be said to have tuned the English tongue; for since its appearance no writer, however deficient in other powers, has wanted melody. Such a series of lines so elaborately corrected and so sweetly modulated took possession of the public ear; the vulgar was enamoured of the poem, and the learned wondered at the translation.

But in the most general applause discordant voices will always be heard. It has been objected by some, who wish to be numbered among the sons of learning, that Pope's version of Homer is not Homerical; that it exhibits no resemblance of the original and characteristic manner of the Father of Poetry, as it wants his awful simplicity, his artless grandeur, his unaffected majesty. This cannot be totally denied; but it must be remembered that *necessitas quod cogit defendit*; that may be lawfully done which cannot be forborne. Time and place will always enforce regard. In estimating this translation consideration must be had of the nature of our language, the form of our metre, and, above all, of the change which two thousand years have made in the modes of life and the habits of thought. Virgil wrote in a language of the same general fabric with that of Homer, in verses of the same measure, and in an age nearer to Homer's time by eighteen hundred years; yet he found even then the state of the world so much altered, and the demand for elegance so much increased, that mere nature would be endured no longer; and perhaps, in the multitude of borrowed passages, very few can be shown which he has not embellished.

There is a time when nations emerging from barbarity, and falling into regular subordination, gain leisure to grow wise, and feel the shame of ignorance and the craving pain of unsatisfied curiosity. To this hunger of the mind plain sense is grateful; that which fills the void removes uneasiness, and to be free from pain for a while is pleasure; but repletion generates fastidiousness, a saturated intellect soon becomes luxurious, and knowledge finds no willing reception till it is recommended by artificial diction. Thus it will be found in the progress of learning that in all nations the first writers are simple, and that every age improves in elegance. One refinement always makes way for another, and what was expedient to Virgil was necessary to Pope.

I suppose many readers of the English *Iliad*, when they have been touched with some unexpected beauty of the lighter kind, have tried to enjoy it in the original, where, alas! it was not to be found. Homer doubtless owes to his translator many Ovidian graces not exactly suitable to his character; but to have added can be no great crime if nothing be taken away. Elegance is surely to be desired if it be not gained at the expense of dignity. A hero would wish to be loved as well as to be reverenced.

To a thousand cavils one answer is sufficient; the purpose of a writer is to be read, and the criticism which would destroy the power of pleasing must be blown aside. Pope wrote for his own age and his own nation: he knew that it was necessary to colour the images and point the sentiments of his author; he therefore made him graceful, but lost him some of his sublimity. . . .

The Epistle to Arbuthnot, now arbitrarily called the *Prologue to the Satires*, is a performance consisting, as it seems, of many fragments wrought into one design, which by this union of scattered beauties contains more striking paragraphs than could probably have been brought together into an occasional work. As there is no stronger motive to exertion than self-defence, no part has more elegance, spirit, or dignity than the poet's vindication of his own character. The meanest passage is the satire upon Sporus.

Of the two poems which derived their names from the year, and which are called the *Epilogue to the Satires*, it was very justly remarked by Savage that the second was in the whole more strongly conceived and more equally supported, but that it had no single passages equal to the contention in the first for the dignity of Vice and the celebration of the triumph of Corruption.

The Imitations of Horace seem to have been written as relaxations of his genius. This employment became his favourite by its facility; the plan was ready to his hand, and nothing was required but to accommodate as he could the sentiments of an old author to recent facts or familiar images; but what is easy is seldom excellent; such imitations cannot give pleasure to common readers; the man of learning may be sometimes surprised and delighted by an unexpected parallel; but the comparison requires knowledge of the original, which will likewise often detect strained applications. Between Roman images and English manners there will be an irreconcileable dissimilitude, and the work will be generally uncouth and party-coloured; neither original nor translated, neither ancient nor modern.

Pope had, in proportions very nicely adjusted to each

other, all the qualities that constitute genius. He had Invention, by which new trains of events are formed and new scenes of imagery displayed, as in *The Rape of the Lock,* and by which extrinsic and adventitious embellishments and illustrations are connected with a known subject, as in the *Essay on Criticism.* He had Imagination, which strongly impresses on the writer's mind and enables him to convey to the reader the various forms of nature, incidents of life, and energies of passion, as in his *Eloisa, Windsor Forest,* and the *Ethick Epistles.* He had Judgement, which selects from life or nature what the present purpose requires, and, by separating the essence of things from its concomitants, often makes the representation more powerful than the reality; and he had colours of language always before him, ready to decorate his matter with every grace of elegant expression, as when he accommodates his diction to the wonderful multiplicity of Homer's sentiments and descriptions.

Poetical expression includes sound as well as meaning. 'Musick', says Dryden, 'is inarticulate poetry'; among the excellences of Pope, therefore, must be mentioned the melody of his metre. By perusing the works of Dryden he discovered the most perfect fabric of English verse, and habituated himself to that only which he found the best; in consequence of which restraint his poetry has been censured as too uniformly musical, and as glutting the ear with unvaried sweetness. I suspect this objection to be the cant of those who judge by principles rather than perception; and who would even themselves have less pleasure in his works if he had tried to relieve attention by studied discords, or affected to break his lines and vary his pauses.

But though he was thus careful of his versification, he did not oppress his powers with superfluous rigour. He seems to have thought with Boileau that the practice of writing might be refined till the difficulty should overbalance the advantage. The construction of his language is not always strictly grammatical; with those rhymes which prescription had conjoined he contented himself, without regard to Swift's remonstrances, though there was no striking consonance; nor was he very careful to vary his terminations or to refuse admission at a small distance to the same rhymes.

To Swift's edict for the exclusion of alexandrines and triplets he paid little regard; he admitted them, but, in the opinion of Fenton, too rarely; he uses them more liberally in his translation than his poems. . . .

It is remarked by Watts that there is scarcely a happy combination of words or a phrase poetically elegant in the English language which Pope has not inserted into his version of Homer. How he obtained possession of so many beauties of speech it were desirable to know. That he gleaned from authors, obscure as well as eminent, what he thought brilliant or useful, and preserved it all in a regular collection, is not unlikely. When, in his last years, Hall's Satires were shown him he wished that he had seen them sooner.

New sentiments and new images others may produce; but to attempt any further improvement of versification will be dangerous. Art and diligence have now done their best, and what shall be added will be the effort of tedious toil and needless curiosity.

After all this it is surely superfluous to answer the question that has once been asked, Whether Pope was a poet? otherwise than by asking in return, If Pope be not a poet, where is poetry to be found? To circumscribe poetry by a definition will only show the narrowness of the definer, though a definition which shall exclude Pope will not easily be made. Let us look round upon the present time, and back upon the past; let us inquire to whom the voice of mankind has decreed the wreath of poetry; let their productions be examined and their claims stated, and the pretensions of Pope will be no more disputed. Had he given the world only his version, the name of poet must have been allowed him: if the writer of the *Iliad* were to class his successors, he would assign a very high place to his translator, without requiring any other evidence of Genius.

From COLERIDGE'S
Biographia Literaria

1817

AMONG those with whom I conversed, there were, of course, very many who had formed their taste, and their notions of poetry, from the writings of Mr. Pope and his followers: or to speak more generally, in that school of French poetry, condensed and invigorated by English understanding, which had predominated from the last century. I was not blind to the merits of this school, yet as from inexperience of the world, and consequent want of sympathy with the general subjects of these poems, they gave me little pleasure, I doubtless undervalued the *kind*, and with the presumption of youth withheld from its masters the legitimate name of poets. I saw that the excellence of this kind consisted in just and acute observations on men and manners in an artificial state of society, as its matter and substance: and in the logic of wit, conveyed in smooth and strong epigrammatic couplets, as its *form*. Even when the subject was addressed to the fancy, or the intellect, as in the *Rape of the Lock*, or the *Essay on Man*; nay, when it was a consecutive narration, as in that astonishing product of matchless talent and ingenuity, Pope's Translation of the *Iliad*; still a *point* was looked for at the end of each second line, and the whole was as it were a sorites, or, if I may exchange a logical for a grammatical metaphor, a *conjunction disjunctive*, of epigrams. Meantime the matter and diction seemed to me characterized not so much by poetic thoughts, as by thoughts *translated* into the language of poetry.

(*Chapter i*)

In the course of one of my Lectures, I had occasion to point out the almost faultless position and choice of words, in Mr. Pope's *original* compositions, particularly in his Satires and moral Essays, for the purpose of comparing them with his translation of Homer, which I do not stand alone in regarding as the main source of our pseudo-poetic diction. And this, by the by, is an additional confirmation of a remark made, I believe, by Sir Joshua Reynolds, that next to the man who forms and elevates the taste of the public, he that corrupts it, is commonly the greatest genius.

(*Chapter ii*)

From *Lectures on Shakespeare*, 1818

Published in *Literary Remains*, 1836–9

In comparing different poets with each other, we should inquire which have brought into the fullest play our imagination and our reason, or have created the greatest excitement and produced the greatest harmony. If we consider great exquisiteness of language and sweetness of metre alone, it is impossible to deny to Pope the character of a delightful writer; but whether he be a poet, must depend upon our definition of the word; and, doubtless, if everything that pleases be poetry, Pope's satires and epistles must be poetry. This I must say, that poetry, as distinguished from other modes of composition, does not rest in metre, and that it is not poetry, if it make no appeal to our passions or our imagination. One character belongs to all true poets, that they write from a principle within, not originating in anything without; and that the true poet's work in its form, its shapings, and its modifications, is distinguished from all other works that assume to belong to the class of poetry, as a natural from an artificial flower, or as the mimic garden of a child from an enamelled meadow. In the former the flowers are broken from their stems and stuck into the ground; they are beautiful to the eye and fragrant to the sense, but their colours soon fade, and their odour is transient as the smile of the planter;—while the meadow may be visited again and again with renewed delight, its beauty is innate in the soul, and its bloom is of the freshness of nature.

From HAZLITT'S
Lecture on Pope

Lectures on the English Poets, 1818

THE question, whether Pope was a poet, has hardly yet been settled, and is hardly worth settling; for if he was not a great poet, he must have been a great prose writer, that is, he was a great writer of some sort. He was a man of exquisite faculties, and of the most refined taste; and as he chose verse (the most obvious distinction of poetry) as the vehicle to express his ideas, he has generally passed for a poet, and a good one. If, indeed, by a great poet, we mean one who gives the utmost grandeur to our conceptions of nature, or the utmost force to the passions of the heart, Pope was not in this sense a great poet; for the bent, the characteristic power of his mind, lay the clean contrary way; namely, in representing things as they appear to the indifferent observer, stripped of prejudice and passion, as in his Critical Essays; or in representing them in the most contemptible and insignificant point of view, as in his Satires; or in clothing the little with mock-dignity, as in his poems of Fancy; or in adorning the trivial incidents and familiar relations of life with the utmost elegance of expression, and all the flattering illusions of friendship or self-love, as in his Epistles. He was not then distinguished as a poet of lofty enthusiasm, of strong imagination, with a passionate sense of the beauties of nature, or a deep insight into the workings of the heart; but he was a wit, and a critic, a man of sense, of observation, and the world, with a keen relish for the elegances of art, or of nature when embellished by art, a quick tact for propriety of thought and manners as established by the forms and customs of society, a refined sympathy with the sentiments and habitudes of human life, as he felt them within the little circle of his family and friends. He was, in a word, the poet, not of nature, but of art; and the distinction between the two, as well as I can make it out, is this—The poet of nature is one who, from the elements of beauty, of power, and of passion in his own breast, sympathizes with whatever is beautiful, and grand, and impassioned in nature, in its simple majesty, in its immediate appeal to the senses, to the thoughts and hearts of all men; so that the poet of nature, by the truth, and depth, and harmony of his mind, may be said to hold communion with the very soul of nature; to be identified with and to foreknow and to record the feelings of all men at all times and places, as they are liable to the same impressions; and to exert the same power over the minds of his readers, that nature does. He sees things in their eternal beauty, for he sees them as they are; he feels them in their universal interest, for he feels them as they affect the first principles of his and our common nature. Such was Homer, such was Shakespeare, whose works will last as long as nature, because they are a copy of the indestructible forms and everlasting impulses of nature, welling out from the bosom as from a perennial spring, or stamped upon the senses by the hand of their maker. The power of the imagination in them, is the representative power of all nature. It has its centre in the human soul, and makes the circuit of the universe.

Pope was not assuredly a poet of this class, or in the first rank of it. He saw nature only dressed by art; he judged of beauty by fashion; he sought for truth in the opinions of the world; he judged of the feelings of others by his own. The capacious soul of Shakespeare had an intuitive and mighty sympathy with whatever could enter into the heart of man in all possible circumstances: Pope had an exact knowledge of all that he himself loved or hated, wished or wanted.

Yet within this retired and narrow circle how much, and that how exquisite, was contained! What discrimination, what wit, what delicacy, what fancy, what lurking spleen, what elegance of thought, what pampered refinement of sentiment! It is like looking at the world through a microscope, where everything assumes a new character and a new consequence, where things are seen in their minutest circumstances and slightest shades of difference; where the little becomes gigantic, the deformed beautiful, and the beautiful deformed. The wrong end of the magnifier is, to be sure, held to everything, but still the exhibition is highly curious, and we know not whether to be most pleased or surprised. Such, at least, is the best account I am able to give of this extraordinary man, without doing injustice to him or others. It is time to refer to particular instances in his works.—The *Rape of the Lock* is the best or most ingenious of these. It is the most exquisite specimen of *filigree* work ever invented. It is admirable in proportion as it is made of nothing.

> More subtle web Arachne cannot spin,
> Nor the fine nets, which oft we woven see
> Of scorched dew, do not in th' air more lightly flee.

It is made of gauze and silver spangles. The most glittering appearance is given to everything, to paste, pomatum, billet-doux, and patches. Airs, languid airs, breathe around;—the atmosphere is perfumed with affectation. A toilette is described with the solemnity of an altar raised to the Goddess of vanity, and the history of a silver bodkin is given with all the pomp of heraldry. No pains are spared, no profusion of ornament, no splendour of poetic diction, to set off the meanest things. The balance between the concealed irony and the assumed gravity, is as nicely trimmed as the balance of power in Europe. The little is made great, and the great little. You hardly know whether to laugh or weep. It is the triumph of insignificance, the apotheosis of foppery and folly. It is the perfection of the mock-heroic!

The finest piece of personal satire in Pope (perhaps in the world) is his character of Addison; and this, it may be observed, is of a mixed kind, made up of his respect for the man, and a cutting sense of his failings. The other finest one is that of Buckingham, and the best part of that is the pleasurable.

—— Alas! how changed from him,
That life of pleasure and that soul of whim:
Gallant and gay, in Cliveden's proud alcove,
The bower of wanton Shrewsbury and love!

Among his happiest and most inimitable effusions are the Epistles to Arbuthnot, and to Jervas the painter; amiable patterns of the delightful unconcerned life, blending ease with dignity, which poets and painters then led. [*Hazlitt here quotes ll.* 125–46 *of the Epistle to Arbuthnot.*]

I cannot help giving also the conclusion of the Epistle to Jervas.

Oh, lasting as those colours may they shine,
Free as thy stroke, yet faultless as thy line;
New graces yearly like thy works display,
Soft without weakness, without glaring gay;

Led by some rule, that guides, but not constrains;
And finish'd more through happiness than pains.
The kindred arts shall in their praise conspire,
One dip the pencil, and one string the lyre.
Yet should the Graces all thy figures place,
And breathe an air divine on ev'ry face;
Yet should the Muses bid my numbers roll
Strong as their charms, and gentle as their soul;
With Zeuxis' Helen thy Bridgewater vie,
And these be sung till Granville's Myra die:
Alas! how little from the grave we claim!
Thou but preserv'st a face, and I a name.

And shall we cut ourselves off from beauties like these with a theory? Shall we shut up our books, and seal up our senses, to please the dull spite and inordinate vanity of those 'who have eyes, but they see not—ears, but they hear not—and understandings, but they understand not',—and go about asking our blind guides, whether Pope was a poet or not? It will never do. Such persons, when you point out to them a fine passage in Pope, turn it off to something of the same sort in some other writer. Thus they say that the line, 'I lisp'd in numbers, for the numbers came', is pretty, but taken from that of Ovid—*Et quum conabar scribere, versus erat.* They are safe in this mode of criticism: there is no danger of any one's tracing their writings to the classics.

Pope's letters and prose writings neither take away from, nor add to his poetical reputation. There is, occasionally, a littleness of manner, and an unnecessary degree of caution. He appears anxious to say a good thing in every word, as well as every sentence. They, however, give a very favourable idea of his moral character in all respects; and his letters to Atterbury, in his disgrace and exile, do equal honour to both. If I had to choose, there are one or two persons, and but one or two, that I should like to have been better than Pope!

From HAZLITT'S Essay
Of Persons one would wish to have seen

The New Monthly Magazine, January 1826; *Winterslow*, 1850

'I thought', said Ayrton, turning short round upon Lamb, 'that you of the Lake School did not like Pope?'—'Not like Pope! My dear sir, you must be under a mistake—I can read him over and over for ever!'—'Why, certainly, the *Essay on Man* must be allowed to be a masterpiece.'—'It may be so, but I seldom look into it.'—'Oh! then it's his Satires you admire?'—'No, not his Satires, but his friendly Epistles and his compliments.'—'Compliments! I did not know he ever made any.'—'The finest', said Lamb, 'that were ever paid by the wit of man. Each of them is worth an estate for life—nay, is an immortality. There is that superb one to Lord Cornbury:

> Despise low joys, low gains;
> Disdain whatever Cornbury disdains;
> Be virtuous, and be happy for your pains.

Was there ever more artful insinuation of idolatrous praise? And then that noble apotheosis of his friend Lord Mansfield (however little deserved), when, speaking of the House of Lords, he adds:

> Conspicuous scene! another yet is nigh,
> (More silent far) where kings and poets lie;
> Where Murray (long enough his country's pride)
> Shall be no more than Tully or than Hyde.

And with what a fine turn of indignant flattery he addresses Lord Bolingbroke:

> Why rail they then, if but one wreath of mine,
> Oh! all accomplish'd St. John, deck thy shrine?

Or turn', continued Lamb, with a slight hectic on his cheek and his eye glistening, 'to his list of early friends:

> But why then publish? Granville the polite,
> And knowing Walsh, would tell me I could write;

Well-natured Garth inflamed with early praise,
And Congreve loved, and Swift endured my lays:
The courtly Talbot, Somers, Sheffield read,
Ev'n mitred Rochester would nod the head;
And St. John's self (great Dryden's friend before)
Received with open arms one poet more.
Happy my studies, if by these approved!
Happier their author, if by these beloved!
From these the world will judge of men and books,
Not from the Burnets, Oldmixons, and Cooks.'

Here his voice totally failed him, and throwing down the book, he said, 'Do you think I would not wish to have been friends with such a man as this?'

From CAMPBELL'S
Essay on English Poetry

Specimens of the British Poets, 1819

POPE gave our heroic couplet its strictest melody and tersest expression. If his contemporaries forgot other poets in admiring him, let him not be robbed of his just fame on pretence that a part of it was superfluous. The public ear was long fatigued with repetitions of his manner; but if we place ourselves in the situation of those to whom his brilliancy, succinctness, and animation were wholly new, we cannot wonder at their being captivated to the fondest admiration. In order to do justice to Pope, we should forget his imitators, if that were possible; but it is easier to remember than to forget by an effort—to acquire associations than to shake them off. Every one may recollect how often the most beautiful air has palled upon his ear, and grown insipid from being played or sung by vulgar musicians. It is the same thing with regard to Pope's versification. That his peculiar rhythm and manner are the very best in the whole range of our poetry need not be asserted. He has a gracefully peculiar manner, though it is not calculated to be an universal one; and where, indeed, shall we find the style of poetry that could be pronounced an exclusive model for every composer? His pauses have little variety, and his phrases are too much weighed in the balance of antithesis. But let us look to the spirit that points his antithesis, and to the rapid precision of his thoughts, and we shall forgive him for being too antithetic and sententious. . . . That Pope was neither so insensible to the beauties of nature, nor so indistinct in describing them as to forfeit the character of a genuine poet, is what I mean to urge, without exaggerating his picturesqueness. But before speaking of that quality in his writings, I would beg leave to observe, in the first place, that the faculty by which a poet luminously describes objects of art, is essentially the same faculty, which enables him to be a faithful describer of simple nature; in the second place, that nature and art are to a greater degree relative terms in poetical description than is generally recollected; and, thirdly, that artificial objects and manners are of so much importance in fiction, as to make the exquisite description of them no less characteristic of genius than the description of simple physical appearances. The poet is 'creation's heir'. He deepens our social interest in existence. It is surely by the liveliness of the interest which he excites in existence, and not by the class of subjects which he chooses, that we most fairly appreciate the genius or the life of life which is in him. It is no irreverence to the external charms of nature to say, that they are not more important to a poet's study, than the manners and affections of his species. Nature is the poet's goddess; but by nature, no one rightly understands her mere inanimate face—however charming it may be—or the simple landscape painting of trees, clouds, precipices, and flowers. Why then try Pope, or any other poet, exclusively by his powers of describing inanimate phenomena? Nature, in the wide and proper sense of the word, means life in all its circumstances—nature moral as well as external. As the subject of inspired fiction, nature includes artificial forms and manners. Richardson is no less a painter of nature than Homer. Homer himself is a minute describer of works of art; and Milton is full of imagery derived from it. Satan's spear is compared to the pine that makes 'the mast of some great ammiral', and his shield is like the moon, but like the moon artificially seen through the glass of the Tuscan artist. The 'spirit-stirring drum, the ear-piercing fife, the royal banner, and all quality, pride, pomp, and circumstance of glorious war', are all artificial images. When Shakespeare groups into one view the most sublime objects of the universe, he fixes first on 'the cloud-capt towers, the gorgeous palaces, the solemn temples'. Those who have ever witnessed the spectacle of the launching of a ship of the line, will perhaps forgive me for adding this to the examples of the sublime of artificial life. Of that spectacle I can never forget the impression, and of having witnessed it reflected from the faces of ten thousand spectators. They seem yet before me—I sympathize with their deep and silent expectation, and with their final burst of enthusiasm. It was not a vulgar joy, but an affecting national solemnity. When the vast bulwark sprang from her cradle, the calm water on which she swung majestically round gave the imagination a contrast of the stormy element on which she was soon to ride. All the days of battle and the nights of danger which she had to encounter, all the ends of the earth which she had to visit, and all that she had to do and to suffer for her country, rose in awful presentiment before the mind; and when the heart gave her a benediction, it was like one pronounced on a living being. . . . Pope's discrimination lay in the lights and shades of human manners, which are at least as interesting as those of rocks and leaves. In moral eloquence he is for ever *densus et instans sibi*. The mind of a poet employed in concentrating such lines as these descriptive of creative power, which

Builds life on death, on change duration founds,
And bids th' eternal wheels to know their rounds,

might well be excused for not descending to the minutely picturesque. The vindictive personality of his satire is a fault of the man, and not of the poet. But his wit is not all his charm. He glows with passion in the *Epistle of Eloisa*, and displays a lofty feeling much above that of the satirist and the man of the world, in his prologue to *Cato*, and his *Epistle to Lord Oxford*. I know not how to designate the possessor of such gifts but by the name of a genuine poet—

—— qualem vix repperit unum
Millibus in multis hominum consultus Apollo.
AUSONIUS.

BYRON ON POPE

Observations upon an Article in Blackwood's Magazine, 1820

I WILL say nothing of the harmony of Pope and Dryden in comparison, for there is not a living poet (except Rogers, Gifford, Campbell, and Crabbe) who can write an heroic couplet. The fact is, that the exquisite beauty of their versification has withdrawn the public attention from their other excellences, as the vulgar eye will rest more upon the splendour of the uniform than the quality of the troops. It is this very harmony, particularly in Pope, which has raised the vulgar and atrocious cant against him:—because his versification is perfect, it is assumed that it is his only perfection; because his truths are so clear, it is asserted that he has no invention; and because he is always intelligible, it is taken for granted that he has no genius. We are sneeringly told that he is the 'Poet of Reason', as if this was a reason for his being no poet.

Letter on the Rev. W. L. Bowles' Strictures on the Life and Writings of Pope, 1821

I look upon this as the declining age of English poetry; no regard for others, no selfish feeling, can prevent me from seeing this, and expressing the truth. There can be no worse sign for the taste of the times than the depreciation of Pope. It would be better to receive for proof Mr. Cobbett's rough but strong attack upon Shakespeare and Milton, than to allow this smooth and 'candid' undermining of the reputation of the most *perfect* of our poets, and the purest of our moralists. Of his power in the *passions,* in description, in the mock-heroic, I leave others to descant. I take him on his strong ground, as an *ethical* poet: in the former none excel; in the mock-heroic and the ethical, none equal him; and in my mind, the latter is the highest of all poetry, because it does that in *verse,* which the greatest of men have wished to accomplish in prose. If the essence of poetry must be a *lie,* throw it to the dogs, or banish it from your republic, as Plato would have done. He who can reconcile poetry with truth and wisdom, is the only true '*poet*' in its real sense, 'the *maker*', 'the *creator*'—why must this mean the 'liar', the 'feigner', the 'tale teller'? A man may make and create better things than these.... He is the only poet that never shocks; the only poet whose *faultlessness* has been made his reproach. Cast your eye over his productions; consider their extent, and contemplate their variety:—pastoral, passion, mock-heroic, translation, satire, ethics,—all excellent, and often perfect. If his great charm be his *melody,* how comes it that foreigners adore him even in their diluted translations?

From DE QUINCEY'S

Article on Pope

Encyclopædia Britannica, 1837

NOT, therefore, for superior correctness, but for qualities the very same as belong to his most distinguished brethren, is Pope to be considered a great poet: for impassioned thinking, powerful description, pathetic reflection, brilliant narration. His characteristic difference is simply that he carried these powers into a different field, and moved chiefly amongst the social paths of men, and viewed their characters as operating through their manners. And our obligations to him arise chiefly on this ground,—that, having already, in the persons of earlier poets, carried off the palm in all the grander trials of intellectual strength, for the majesty of the epopee and the impassioned vehemence of the tragic drama, to Pope we owe it that we can now claim an equal pre-eminence in the sportive and aerial graces of the mock-heroic and satire muse; that in the *Dunciad* we possess a peculiar form of satire, in which (according to a plan unattempted by any other nation) we see alternately her festive smile and her gloomiest scowl; that the grave good sense of the nation has here found its brightest mirror; and, finally, that through Pope the cycle of our poetry is perfected and made orbicular,—that from that day we might claim the laurel equally, whether for dignity or grace.

Essay on Pope

The North British Review, August 1848

Amongst the early poems of Pope the *Eloisa to Abelard* has a special interest of a double order:—First, it has a *personal* interest as the poem of Pope, because indicating the original destination of Pope's intellect, and the strength of his native vocation to a class of poetry in deeper keys of passion than any which he systematically cultivated. For itself also, and abstracting from its connexion with Pope's natural destination, this poem has a *second* interest, an intrinsic interest, that will always make it dear to impassioned minds. The self-conflict—the flux and reflux of the poor agitated heart—the spectacle of Eloisa now bending penitentially before the shadowy austerities of a monastic future, now raving upon the remembrances of the guilty past—one moment reconciled by the very anguish of her soul to the grandeurs of religion and of prostrate adoration, the next moment revolting to perilous retrospects of her treacherous happiness—the recognition, by shining gleams through the very storms and darkness evoked by her earthly sensibilities, of a sensibility deeper far in its ground, and that trembled towards holier objects—the lyrical tumult of the changes, the hope, the tears, the rapture, the penitence, the despair—place the reader in tumultuous sympathy with the poor distracted nun. Exquisitely imagined, among the passages towards the end, is the introduction of a voice speaking to Eloisa from the grave of some sister nun that, in long-forgotten years, once had struggled and suffered like herself—

> Once (like herself) that trembled, wept, and prayed,
> Love's victim then, though now a sainted maid.

Exquisite is the passage in which she prefigures a visit yet to come from Abelard to herself—no more in the character of a lover, but as a priest, ministering by spiritual consolations to her dying hours, pointing her thoughts to heaven, presenting the Cross to her through the mists of death, and fighting for her as a spiritual ally against the torments of flesh. That anticipation was not gratified. Abelard died long before her; and the hour never arrived for *him* of which with such tenderness she says—

> It will be *then* no crime to gaze on me.

But another anticipation *has* been fulfilled in a degree that she could hardly have contemplated; the anticipation, namely—

> That ages hence, when all her woes were o'er,
> And that rebellious heart should beat no more,

wandering feet should be attracted from afar

> To Paraclete's white walls and silver springs

as the common resting-place and everlasting marriage-bed of Abelard and Eloisa; that the eyes of many who had been touched by their story, by the memory of their extraordinary accomplishments in an age of darkness, and by the calamitous issue of their attachment, should seek, first and last, for the grave in which the lovers trusted to meet again in peace; and should seek it with interest so absorbing that even amidst the ascent of hosannahs from the choir, amidst the grandeurs of high mass, the raising of the host, and 'the pomp of dreadful sacrifice', sometimes these wandering eyes should steal aside to the solemn abiding-place of Abelard and his Eloisa, offering so pathetic a contrast, by its peaceful silence, to the agitations of their lives; and that there, amidst thoughts which by right were all due and dedicated

> to heaven,
> One *human* tear should drop and be forgiven.

Selections from

ALEXANDER POPE'S

POETRY and PROSE

2179.34

D

ODE ON SOLITUDE

Written about 1700; published in
Miscellany Poems, 1726

HAPPY the man, whose wish and care
A few paternal acres bound,
Content to breathe his native air,
In his own ground.

Whose herds with milk, whose fields with bread,
Whose flocks supply him with attire,
Whose trees in summer yield him shade,
In winter fire.

Blest, who can unconcern'dly find
Hours, days, and years slide soft away,
In health of body, peace of mind,
Quiet by day,

Sound sleep by night; study and ease,
Together mixt; sweet recreation;
And innocence, which most does please
With meditation.

Thus let me live, unseen, unknown,
Thus unlamented let me die,
Steal from the world, and not a stone
Tell where I lie.

AN ESSAY ON CRITICISM

1711

Lines 215–383

A *little learning* is a dang'rous thing;
Drink deep, or taste not the Pierian spring:
There shallow draughts intoxicate the brain,
And drinking largely sobers us again.
Fir'd at first sight with what the Muse imparts,
In fearless youth we tempt the heights of Arts,
While from the bounded level of our mind,
Short views we take, nor see the lengths behind;
But more advanc'd, behold with strange surprize
New distant scenes of endless science rise!
So pleas'd at first the tow'ring Alps we try,
Mount o'er the vales, and seem to tread the sky,
Th' eternal snows appear already past,
And the first clouds and mountains seem the last:
But, those attain'd, we tremble to survey
The growing labours of the lengthen'd way,
Th' increasing prospect tires our wand'ring eyes,
Hills peep o'er hills, and Alps on Alps arise!
A perfect Judge will read each work of Wit
With the same spirit that its author writ:
Survey the WHOLE, nor seek slight faults to find
Where nature moves, and rapture warms the mind;
Nor lose, for that malignant dull delight,
The gen'rous pleasure to be charm'd with wit.
But in such lays as neither ebb, nor flow,
Correctly cold, and regularly low,
That shunning faults, one quiet tenour keep;
We cannot blame indeed—but we may sleep.

In Wit, as Nature, what affects our hearts
Is not th' exactness of peculiar parts;
'Tis not a lip, or eye, we beauty call,
But the joint force and full result of all.
Thus when we view some well-proportion'd dome,
(The world's just wonder, and ev'n thine, O Rome!)
No single parts unequally surprize,
All comes united to th' admiring eyes;
No monstrous height, or breadth, or length appear;
The Whole at once is bold, and regular.
Whoever thinks a faultless piece to see,
Thinks what ne'er was, nor is, nor e'er shall be.
In ev'ry work regard the writer's End,
Since none can compass more than they intend;
And if the means be just, the conduct true,
Applause, in spight of trivial faults, is due.
As men of breeding, sometimes men of wit,
T' avoid great errors, must the less commit:
Neglect the rules each verbal Critic lays,
For not to know some trifles, is a praise.
Most Critics, fond of some subservient art,
Still make the Whole depend upon a Part:
They talk of principles, but notions prize,
And all to one lov'd Folly sacrifice.
Once on a time, La Mancha's Knight, they say,
A certain Bard encount'ring on the way,
Discours'd in terms as just, with looks as sage,
As e'er could Dennis, of the Grecian stage;
Concluding all were desp'rate sots and fools,
Who durst depart from Aristotle's rules.
Our Author, happy in a judge so nice,
Produc'd his Play, and begg'd the Knight's advice;
Made him observe the subject, and the plot,
The manners, passions, unities; what not?

All which, exact to rule, were brought about,
Were but a Combat in the lists left out.
'What! leave the Combat out?' exclaims the Knight;
Yes, or we must renounce the Stagirite.
'Not so by Heav'n' (he answers in a rage),
'Knights, squires, and steeds, must enter on the stage.'
So vast a throng the stage can ne'er contain.
'Then build a new, or act it in a plain.'
  Thus Critics, of less judgment than caprice,
Curious not knowing, not exact but nice,
Form short Ideas; and offend in arts
(As most in manners) by a love to parts.
  Some to *Conceit* alone their taste confine,
And glitt'ring thoughts struck out at ev'ry line;
Pleas'd with a work where nothing's just or fit;
One glaring Chaos and wild heap of wit.
Poets like painters, thus, unskill'd to trace
The naked nature and the living grace,
With gold and jewels cover ev'ry part,
And hide with ornaments their want of art.
True Wit is Nature to advantage dress'd,
What oft was thought, but ne'er so well express'd;
Something, whose truth convinc'd at sight we find,
That gives us back the image of our mind.
As shades more sweetly recommend the light,
So modest plainness sets off sprightly wit.
For works may have more wit than does 'em good,
As bodies perish thro' excess of blood.
  Others for *Language* all their care express,
And value books, as women men, for Dress:
Their praise is still,—the Style is excellent:
The Sense, they humbly take upon content.
Words are like leaves; and where they most abound,
Much fruit of sense beneath is rarely found.

False Eloquence, like the prismatic glass,
Its gaudy colours spreads on ev'ry place;
The face of Nature we no more survey,
All glares alike, without distinction gay:
But true Expression, like th' unchanging Sun,
Clears, and improves whate'er it shines upon,
It gilds all objects, but it alters none.
Expression is the dress of thought, and still
Appears more decent, as more suitable;
A vile conceit in pompous words express'd,
Is like a clown in regal purple dress'd:
For diff'rent styles with diff'rent subjects sort,
As several garbs with country, town, and court.
Some by old words to fame have made pretence,
Ancients in phrase, mere moderns in their sense;
Such labour'd nothings, in so strange a style,
Amaze th' unlearn'd, and make the learned smile.
Unlucky, as Fungoso in the Play,
These sparks with aukward vanity display
What the fine gentleman wore yesterday;
And but so mimic ancient wits at best,
As apes our grandsires, in their doublets drest.
In words, as fashions, the same rule will hold;
Alike fantastic, if too new, or old:
Be not the first by whom the new are try'd,
Nor yet the last to lay the old aside.
  But most by Numbers judge a Poet's song;
And smooth or rough, with them, is right or wrong:
In the bright Muse tho' thousand charms conspire,
Her Voice is all these tuneful fools admire;
Who haunt Parnassus but to please their ear,
Not mend their minds; as some to Church repair,
Not for the doctrine, but the music there.
These equal syllables alone require,

Tho' oft the ear the open vowels tire;
While expletives their feeble aid do join;
And ten low words oft creep in one dull line:
While they ring round the same unvary'd chimes,
With sure returns of still expected rhymes;
Where-e'er you find 'the cooling western breeze,'
In the next line, it 'whispers thro' the trees:'
If crystal streams 'with pleasing murmurs creep,'
The reader's threaten'd (not in vain) with 'sleep:'
Then, at the last and only couplet fraught
With some unmeaning thing they call a thought,
A needless Alexandrine ends the song,
That, like a wounded snake, drags its slow length along.
Leave such to tune their own dull rhymes, and know
What's roundly smooth, or languishingly slow;
And praise the easy vigour of a line,
Where Denham's strength, and Waller's sweetness join.
True ease in writing comes from art, not chance,
As those move easiest who have learn'd to dance.
'Tis not enough no harshness gives offence,
The sound must seem an Echo to the sense:
Soft is the strain when Zephyr gently blows,
And the smooth stream in smoother numbers flows;
But when loud surges lash the sounding shoar,
The hoarse, rough verse should like the torrent roar:
When Ajax strives some rock's vast weight to throw,
The line too labours, and the words move slow;
Not so, when swift Camilla scours the plain,
Flies o'er th' unbending corn, and skims along the main.
Hear how Timotheus' vary'd lays surprize,
And bid alternate passions fall and rise!
While, at each change, the son of Libyan Jove
Now burns with glory, and then melts with love;
Now his fierce eyes with sparkling fury glow,

Now sighs steal out, and tears begin to flow:
Persians and Greeks like turns of nature found,
And the World's victor stood subdu'd by Sound!
The pow'r of Music all our hearts allow,
And what Timotheus was, is DRYDEN now.

THE

RAPE of the *LOCK*.

AN

HEROI-COMICAL

POEM.

In FIVE CANTO'S.

Written by Mr. *POPE*.

——*A tonso est hoc nomen adepta capillo.*
OVID.

LONDON:
Printed for BERNARD LINTOTT, at the *Cross-Keys* in *Fleetstreet*. 1714.

The Rape of the Lock

To Mrs. ARABELLA FERMOR

MADAM,

It will be in vain to deny that I have some regard for this piece, since I dedicate it to You. Yet you may bear me witness, it was intended only to divert a few young Ladies, who have good sense and good humour enough to laugh not only at their sex's little unguarded follies, but at their own. But as it was communicated with the air of a Secret, it soon found its way into the world. An imperfect copy having been offer'd to a Bookseller, you had the good-nature for my sake to consent to the publication of one more correct: This I was forc'd to, before I had executed half my design, for the Machinery was entirely wanting to compleat it.

The Machinery, Madam, is a term invented by the Critics, to signify that part which the Deities, Angels, or Dæmons are made to act in a Poem: For the ancient Poets are in one respect like many modern Ladies: let an action be never so trivial in itself, they always make it appear of the utmost importance. These Machines I determin'd to raise on a very new and odd foundation, the Rosicrucian doctrine of Spirits.

I know how disagreeable it is to make use of hard words before a Lady; but 'tis so much the concern of a Poet to have his works understood, and particularly by your Sex, that you must give me leave to explain two or three difficult terms.

The Rosicrucians are a people I must bring you acquainted with. The best account I know of them is in a French book call'd *Le Comte de Gabalis,* which both in its title and size is so like a Novel, that many of the Fair Sex have read it for one by mistake. According to these Gentlemen, the four

Elements are inhabited by Spirits, which they call Sylphs, Gnomes, Nymphs, and Salamanders. The Gnomes or Dæmons of Earth delight in mischief; but the Sylphs, whose habitation is in the Air, are the best-condition'd creatures imaginable. For they say, any mortals may enjoy the most intimate familiarities with these gentle Spirits, upon a condition very easy to all true Adepts, an inviolate preservation of Chastity.

As to the following Cantos, all the passages of them are as fabulous, as the Vision at the beginning, or the Transformation at the end; (except the loss of your Hair, which I always mention with reverence.) The Human persons are as fictitious as the Airy ones; and the character of Belinda, as it is now manag'd, resembles you in nothing but in Beauty.

If this Poem had as many Graces as there are in your Person, or in your Mind, yet I could never hope it should pass thro' the world half so Uncensur'd as You have done. But let its fortune be what it will, mine is happy enough, to have given me this occasion of assuring you that I am, with the truest esteem,

MADAM,

Your most obedient, Humble Servant,

A. POPE.

Nolueram, Belinda, tuos violare capillos;
Sed juvat, hoc precibus me tribuisse tuis. MART.

CANTO I

WHAT dire offence from am'rous causes springs,
What mighty contests rise from trivial things,
I sing—This verse to CARYL, Muse! is due:
This, ev'n Belinda may vouchsafe to view:
Slight is the subject, but not so the praise,
If She inspire, and He approve my lays.

Say what strange motive, Goddess! could compel
A well-bred Lord t' assault a gentle Belle?
Oh say what stranger cause, yet unexplor'd,
Could make a gentle Belle reject a Lord?
In talks so bold, can little men engage,
And in soft bosoms dwells such mighty Rage?
Sol thro' white curtains shot a tim'rous ray,
And ope'd those eyes that must eclipse the day:
Now lap-dogs give themselves the rousing shake,
And sleepless lovers, just at twelve, awake:
Thrice rung the bell, the slipper knock'd the ground,
And the press'd watch return'd a silver sound.
Belinda still her downy pillow prest,
Her guardian SYLPH prolong'd the balmy rest:
'Twas He had summon'd to her silent bed
The morning-dream that hover'd o'er her head;
A Youth more glitt'ring than a Birth-night Beau,
(That ev'n in slumber caus'd her cheek to glow)
Seem'd to her ear his winning lips to lay,
And thus in whispers said, or seem'd to say.
Fairest of mortals, thou distinguish'd care
Of thousand bright Inhabitants of Air!
If e'er one Vision touch thy infant thought,
Of all the Nurse and all the Priest have taught;
Of airy Elves by moonlight shadows seen,
The silver token, and the circled green,
Or virgins visited by Angel-pow'rs,
With golden crowns and wreaths of heav'nly flow'rs;
Hear and believe! thy own importance know,
Nor bound thy narrow views to things below.
Some secret truths, from learned pride conceal'd,
To Maids alone and Children are reveal'd:
What tho' no credit doubting Wits may give?
The Fair and Innocent shall still believe.

Know then, unnumber'd Spirits round thee fly,
The light Militia of the lower sky:
These, tho' unseen, are ever on the wing,
Hang o'er the Box, and hover round the Ring.
Think what an equipage thou hast in Air,
And view with scorn two Pages and a Chair.
As now your own, our beings were of old,
And once inclos'd in Woman's beauteous mould;
Thence, by a soft transition, we repair
From earthly Vehicles to these of air.
Think not, when Woman's transient breath is fled,
That all her vanities at once are dead;
Succeeding vanities she still regards,
And tho' she plays no more, o'erlooks the cards.
Her joy in gilded Chariots, when alive,
And love of Ombre, after death survive.
For when the Fair in all their pride expire,
To their first Elements their Souls retire:
The Sprites of fiery Termagants in Flame
Mount up, and take a Salamander's name.
Soft yielding minds to Water glide away,
And sip, with Nymphs, their elemental Tea.
The graver Prude sinks downward to a Gnome,
In search of mischief still on Earth to roam.
The light Coquettes in Sylphs aloft repair,
And sport and flutter in the fields of Air.
  Know farther yet; whoever fair and chaste
Rejects mankind, is by some Sylph embrac'd:
For Spirits, freed from mortal laws, with ease
Assume what sexes and what shapes they please.
What guards the purity of melting Maids,
In courtly balls, and midnight masquerades,
Safe from the treach'rous friend, the daring spark,
The glance by day, the whisper in the dark,

When kind occasion prompts their warm desires,
When music softens, and when dancing fires?
'Tis but their Sylph, the wise Celestials know,
Tho' Honour is the word with Men below.
Some nymphs there are, too conscious of their face,
For life predestin'd to the Gnomes embrace.
These swell their prospects and exalt their pride,
When offers are disdain'd, and love deny'd:
Then gay Ideas croud the vacant brain,
While Peers, and Dukes, and all their sweeping train,
And Garters, Stars, and Coronets appear,
And in soft sounds, Your Grace salutes their ear.
'Tis these that early taint the female soul,
Instruct the eyes of young Coquettes to roll,
Teach Infant-cheeks a bidden blush to know,
And little hearts to flutter at a Beau.
Oft, when the world imagine women stray,
The Sylphs thro' mystic mazes guide their way,
Thro' all the giddy circle they pursue,
And old impertinence expel by new.
What tender maid but must a victim fall
To one man's treat, but for another's ball?
When Florio speaks what virgin could withstand,
If gentle Damon did not squeeze her hand?
With varying vanities, from ev'ry part,
They shift the moving Toyshop of their heart;
Where wigs with wigs, with sword-knots sword-knots strive,
Beaux banish beaux, and coaches coaches drive.
This erring mortals Levity may call,
Oh blind to truth! the Sylphs contrive it all.
Of these am I, who thy protection claim,
A watchful sprite, and Ariel is my name.
Late, as I rang'd the crystal wilds of air,
In the clear Mirror of thy ruling Star

I saw, alas! some dread event impend,
Ere to the main this morning sun descend,
But heav'n reveals not what, or how, or where:
Warn'd by the Sylph, oh pious maid, beware!
This to disclose is all thy guardian can:
Beware of all, but most beware of Man!
  He said; when Shock, who thought she slept too long,
Leap'd up, and wak'd his mistress with his tongue.
'Twas then Belinda, if report say true,
Thy eyes first open'd on a Billet-doux;
Wounds, Charms, and Ardors, were no sooner read,
But all the Vision vanish'd from thy head.
  And now, unveil'd, the Toilet stands display'd,
Each silver Vase in mystic order laid.
First, rob'd in white, the Nymph intent adores,
With head uncover'd, the Cosmetic pow'rs.
A heav'nly Image in the glass appears,
To that she bends, to that her eyes she rears;
Th' inferior Priestess, at her altar's side,
Trembling, begins the sacred rites of Pride.
Unnumber'd treasures ope at once, and here
The various off'rings of the world appear;
From each she nicely culls with curious toil,
And decks the Goddess with the glitt'ring spoil.
This casket India's glowing gems unlocks,
And all Arabia breathes from yonder box.
The Tortoise here and Elephant unite,
Transform'd to combs, the speckled, and the white.
Here files of pins extend their shining rows,
Puffs, Powders, Patches, Bibles, Billet-doux.
Now awful Beauty puts on all its arms;
The fair each moment rises in her charms,
Repairs her smiles, awakens ev'ry grace,
And calls forth all the wonders of her face;

Sees by degrees a purer blush arise,
And keener lightnings quicken in her eyes.
The busy Sylphs surround their darling care,
These set the head, and those divide the hair,
Some fold the sleeve, whilst others plait the gown;
And Betty's prais'd for labours not her own.

CANTO II

Not with more glories, in th' etherial plain,
The Sun first rises o'er the purpled main,
Than, issuing forth, the rival of his beams
Launch'd on the bosom of the silver Thames.
Fair Nymphs, and well-drest Youths around her shone,
But ev'ry eye was fix'd on her alone.
On her white breast a sparkling Cross she wore,
Which Jews might kiss, and Infidels adore.
Her lively looks a sprightly mind disclose,
Quick as her eyes, and as unfix'd as those:
Favours to none, to all she smiles extends;
Oft she rejects, but never once offends.
Bright as the sun, her eyes the gazers strike,
And, like the sun, they shine on all alike.
Yet graceful ease, and sweetness void of pride
Might hide her faults, if Belles had faults to hide:
If to her share some female errors fall,
Look on her face, and you'll forget 'em all.
  This Nymph, to the destruction of mankind,
Nourish'd two Locks, which graceful hung behind
In equal curls, and well conspir'd to deck
With shining ringlets the smooth iv'ry neck.
Love in these labyrinths his slaves detains,
And mighty hearts are held in slender chains.
With hairy springes we the birds betray,
Slight lines of hair surprize the finny prey,

Fair tresses man's imperial race insnare,
And beauty draws us with a single hair.
  Th' advent'rous Baron the bright locks admir'd;
He saw, he wish'd, and to the prize aspir'd.
Resolv'd to win, he meditates the way,
By force to ravish, or by fraud betray;
For when success a Lover's toil attends,
Few ask, if fraud or force attain'd his ends.
  For this, ere Phœbus rose, he had implor'd
Propitious heav'n, and ev'ry pow'r ador'd,
But chiefly Love—to Love an Altar built,
Of twelve vast French Romances, neatly gilt.
There lay three garters, half a pair of gloves;
And all the trophies of his former loves;
With tender Billet-doux he lights the pyre,
And breathes three am'rous sighs to raise the fire.
Then prostrate falls, and begs with ardent eyes
Soon to obtain, and long possess the prize:
The pow'rs gave ear, and granted half his pray'r,
The rest, the winds dispers'd in empty air.
  But now secure the painted vessel glides,
The sun-beams trembling on the floating tides:
While melting music steals upon the sky,
And soften'd sounds along the waters die;
Smooth flow the waves, the Zephyrs gently play,
Belinda smil'd, and all the world was gay.
All but the Sylph—with careful thoughts opprest,
Th' impending woe sat heavy on his breast.
He summons strait his Denizens of air;
The lucid squadrons round the sails repair;
Soft o'er the shrouds aërial whispers breathe,
That seem'd but Zephyrs to the train beneath.
Some to the sun their insect-wings unfold,
Waft on the breeze, or sink in clouds of gold;

Transparent forms, too fine for mortal sight,
Their fluid bodies half dissolv'd in light.
Loose to the wind their airy garments flew,
Thin glitt'ring textures of the filmy dew,
Dipt in the richest tincture of the skies,
Where light disports in ever-mingling dyes,
While ev'ry beam new transient colours flings,
Colours that change whene'er they wave their wings.
Amid the circle, on the gilded mast,
Superior by the head, was Ariel plac'd;
His purple pinions op'ning to the sun,
He rais'd his azure wand, and thus begun.
  Ye Sylphs and Sylphids, to your chief give ear,
Fays, Fairies, Genii, Elves, and Dæmons hear!
Ye know the spheres and various tasks assign'd
By laws eternal to th' aërial kind.
Some in the fields of purest Æther play,
And bask and whiten in the blaze of day.
Some guide the course of wand'ring orbs on high,
Or roll the planets thro' the boundless sky.
Some less refin'd, beneath the moon's pale light
Pursue the stars that shoot athwart the night,
Or suck the mists in grosser air below,
Or dip their pinions in the painted bow,
Or brew fierce tempests on the wintry main,
Or o'er the glebe distil the kindly rain.
Others on earth o'er human race preside,
Watch all their ways, and all their actions guide:
Of these the chief the care of Nations own,
And guard with Arms divine the British Throne.
  Our humbler province is to tend the Fair,
Not a less pleasing, tho' less glorious care;
To save the powder from too rude a gale,
Nor let th' imprison'd essences exhale;

To draw fresh colours from the vernal flow'rs;
To steal from rainbows e'er they drop in show'rs
A brighter wash; to curl their waving hairs,
Assist their blushes, and inspire their airs;
Nay oft, in dreams, invention we bestow,
To change a Flounce, or add a Furbelow.
  This day, black Omens threat the brightest Fair
That e'er deserv'd a watchful spirit's care;
Some dire disaster, or by force, or slight;
But what, or where, the fates have wrapt in night.
Whether the nymph shall break Diana's law,
Or some frail China jar receive a flaw;
Or stain her honour, or her new brocade;
Forget her pray'rs, or miss a masquerade;
Or lose her heart, or necklace, at a ball;
Or whether Heav'n has doom'd that Shock must fall.
Haste then, ye spirits! to your charge repair:
The flutt'ring fan be Zephyretta's care;
The drops to thee, Brillante, we consign;
And, Momentilla, let the watch be thine;
Do thou, Crispissa, tend her fav'rite Lock;
Ariel himself shall be the guard of Shock.
  To fifty chosen Sylphs, of special note,
We trust th' important charge, the Petticoat:
Oft have we known that seven-fold fence to fail,
Tho' stiff with hoops, and arm'd with ribs of whale;
Form a strong line about the silver bound,
And guard the wide circumference around.
  Whatever spirit, careless of his charge,
His post neglects, or leaves the fair at large,
Shall feel sharp vengeance soon o'ertake his sins,
Be stop'd in vials, or transfix'd with pins;
Or plung'd in lakes of bitter washes lie,
Or wedg'd whole ages in a bodkin's eye:

Gums and Pomatums shall his flight restrain,
While clog'd he beats his silken wings in vain;
Or Alum styptics with contracting pow'r
Shrink his thin essence like a rivel'd flow'r:
Or, as Ixion fix'd, the wretch shall feel
The giddy motion of the whirling Mill,
In fumes of burning Chocolate shall glow,
And tremble at the sea that froths below!
He spoke; the spirits from the sails descend;
Some, orb in orb, around the nymph extend;
Some thrid the mazy ringlets of her hair;
Some hang upon the pendants of her ear;
With beating hearts the dire event they wait,
Anxious, and trembling for the birth of Fate.

CANTO III

Close by those meads, for ever crown'd with flow'rs,
Where Thames with pride surveys his rising tow'rs,
There stands a structure of majestic frame,
Which from the neighb'ring Hampton takes its name.
Here Britain's statesmen oft the fall foredoom
Of foreign Tyrants, and of Nymphs at home;
Here thou, great ANNA! whom three realms obey,
Dost sometimes counsel take—and sometimes Tea.
Hither the heroes and the nymphs resort,
To taste awhile the pleasures of a Court;
In various talk th' instructive hours they past,
Who gave the ball, or paid the visit last;
One speaks the glory of the British Queen,
And one describes a charming Indian screen;
A third interprets motions, looks, and eyes;
At ev'ry word a reputation dies.
Snuff, or the fan, supply each pause of chat,
With singing, laughing, ogling, *and all that.*

Mean while, declining from the noon of day,
The sun obliquely shoots his burning ray;
The hungry Judges soon the sentence sign,
And wretches hang that jury-men may dine;
The merchant from th' Exchange returns in peace,
And the long labours of the Toilet cease.
Belinda now, whom thirst of fame invites,
Burns to encounter two advent'rous Knights,
At Ombre singly to decide their doom;
And swells her breast with conquests yet to come.
Strait the three bands prepare in arms to join,
Each band the number of the sacred nine.
Soon as she spreads her hand, th' aërial guard
Descend, and sit on each important card:
First Ariel perch'd upon a Matadore,
Then each, according to the rank they bore;
For Sylphs, yet mindful of their ancient race,
Are, as when women, wondrous fond of place.
Behold, four Kings in majesty rever'd,
With hoary whiskers and a forky beard;
And four fair Queens whose hands sustain a flow'r,
Th' expressive emblem of their softer pow'r;
Four Knaves in garbs succinct, a trusty band,
Caps on their heads, and halberts in their hand;
And particolour'd troops, a shining train,
Draw forth to combat on the velvet plain.
The skilful Nymph reviews her force with care:
Let Spades be trumps! she said, and trumps they were.
Now move to war her sable Matadores,
In show like leaders of the swarthy Moors.
Spadillio first, unconquerable Lord!
Led off two captive trumps, and swept the board.
As many more Manillio forc'd to yield,
And march'd a victor from the verdant field.

Him Basto follow'd, but his fate more hard
Gain'd but one trump and one Plebeian card.
With his broad sabre next, a chief in years,
The hoary Majesty of Spades appears,
Puts forth one manly leg, to sight reveal'd,
The rest, his many-colour'd robe conceal'd.
The rebel Knave, who dares his prince engage,
Proves the just victim of his royal rage.
Ev'n mighty Pam, that Kings and Queens o'erthrew
And mow'd down armies in the fights of Lu,
Sad chance of war! now destitute of aid,
Falls undistinguished by the victor Spade!
  Thus far both armies to Belinda yield;
Now to the Baron fate inclines the field.
His warlike Amazon her host invades,
Th' imperial consort of the crown of Spades.
The Club's black Tyrant first her victim dy'd,
Spite of his haughty mien, and barb'rous pride:
What boots the regal circle on his head,
His giant limbs, in state unwieldy spread;
That long behind he trails his pompous robe,
And, of all monarchs, only grasps the globe?
  The Baron now his Diamonds pours apace;
Th' embroider'd King who shows but half his face,
And his refulgent Queen, with pow'rs combin'd
Of broken troops an easy conquest find.
Clubs, Diamonds, Hearts, in wild disorder seen,
With throngs promiscuous strow the level green.
Thus when dispers'd a routed army runs,
Of Asia's troops, and Afric's sable sons,
With like confusion different nations fly,
Of various habit, and of various dye;
The pierc'd battalions dis-united fall,
In heaps on heaps; one fate o'erwhelms them all.

The Knave of Diamonds tries his wily arts,
And wins (oh shameful chance!) the queen of Hearts.
At this, the blood the virgin's cheek forsook,
A livid paleness spreads o'er all her look;
She sees, and trembles at th' approaching ill,
Just in the jaws of ruin, and Codille.
And now (as oft in some distemper'd State)
On one nice Trick depends the gen'ral fate.
An Ace of Hearts steps forth: The King unseen
Lurk'd in her hand, and mourn'd his captive Queen:
He springs to vengeance with an eager pace,
And falls like thunder on the prostrate Ace.
The nymph exulting fills with shouts the sky;
The walls, the woods, and long canals reply.
Oh thoughtless mortals! ever blind to fate,
Too soon dejected, and too soon elate.
Sudden, these honours shall be snatch'd away,
And curs'd for ever this victorious day.
For lo! the board with cups and spoons is crown'd,
The berries crackle, and the mill turns round;
On shining Altars of Japan they raise
The silver lamp; the fiery spirits blaze:
From silver spouts the grateful liquors glide,
While China's earth receives the smoaking tide:
At once they gratify their scent and taste,
And frequent cups prolong the rich repaste.
Strait hover round the Fair her airy band;
Some, as she sipp'd, the fuming liquor fann'd,
Some o'er her lap their careful plumes display'd,
Trembling, and conscious of the rich brocade.
Coffee (which makes the politician wise,
And see thro' all things with his half-shut eyes)
Sent up in vapours to the Baron's brain
New stratagems, the radiant Lock to gain.

Ah cease, rash youth! desist ere 'tis too late,
Fear the just Gods, and think of Scylla's Fate!
Chang'd to a bird, and sent to flit in air,
She dearly pays for Nisus' injur'd hair!
  But when to mischief mortals bend their will,
How soon they find fit instruments of ill!
Just then, Clarissa drew with tempting grace
A two-edg'd weapon from her shining case:
So Ladies in Romance assist their Knight,
Present the spear, and arm him for the fight.
He takes the gift with rev'rence, and extends
The little engine on his fingers' ends;
This just behind Belinda's neck he spread,
As o'er the fragrant steams she bends her head.
Swift to the Lock a thousand Sprites repair,
A thousand wings, by turns, blow back the hair;
And thrice they twitch'd the diamond in her ear;
Thrice she look'd back, and thrice the foe drew near.
Just in that instant, anxious Ariel sought
The close recesses of the Virgin's thought;
As on the nosegay in her breast reclin'd,
He watch'd th' Ideas rising in her mind,
Sudden he view'd, in spite of all her art,
An earthly Lover lurking at her heart.
Amaz'd, confus'd, he found his pow'r expir'd,
Resign'd to fate, and with a sigh retir'd.
  The Peer now spreads the glitt'ring Forfex wide,
T' inclose the Lock; now joins it, to divide.
Ev'n then, before the fatal engine clos'd,
A wretched Sylph too fondly interpos'd;
Fate urg'd the sheers, and cut the Sylph in twain,
(But airy substance soon unites again)
The meeting points the sacred hair dissever
From the fair head, for ever, and for ever!

Then flash'd the living lightning from her eyes,
And screams of horror rend th' affrighted skies.
Not louder shrieks to pitying heav'n are cast,
When husbands, or when lap-dogs breathe their last;
Or when rich China vessels, fall'n from high,
In glitt'ring dust, and painted fragments lie!
Let wreaths of triumph now my temples twine,
(The Victor cry'd) the glorious Prize is mine!
While fish in streams, or birds delight in air,
Or in a coach and six the British Fair,
As long as Atalantis shall be read,
Or the small pillow grace a Lady's bed,
While visits shall be paid on solemn days,
When num'rous wax-lights in bright order blaze,
While nymphs take treats, or assignations give,
So long my honour, name, and praise shall live!
What Time would spare, from Steel receives its date,
And monuments, like men, submit to fate!
Steel could the labour of the Gods destroy,
And strike to dust th' imperial tow'rs of Troy;
Steel could the works of mortal pride confound,
And hew triumphal arches to the ground.
What wonder then, fair nymph! thy hairs should feel,
The conqu'ring force of unresisted steel?

CANTO IV

But anxious cares the pensive nymph oppress'd,
And secret passions labour'd in her breast.
Not youthful kings in battle seiz'd alive,
Not scornful virgins who their charms survive,
Not ardent lovers robb'd of all their bliss,
Not ancient ladies when refus'd a kiss,
Not tyrants fierce that unrepenting die,
Not Cynthia when her manteau's pinn'd awry,

E'er felt such rage, resentment, and despair,
As thou, sad Virgin! for thy ravish'd Hair.
For, that sad moment, when the Sylphs withdrew,
And Ariel weeping from Belinda flew,
Umbriel, a dusky, melancholy sprite,
As ever sully'd the fair face of light,
Down to the central earth, his proper scene,
Repair'd to search the gloomy Cave of Spleen.
Swift on his sooty pinions flits the Gnome,
And in a vapour reach'd the dismal dome.
No chearful breeze this sullen region knows,
The dreaded East is all the wind that blows.
Here in a grotto, shelter'd close from air,
And screen'd in shades from day's detested glare,
She sighs for ever on her pensive bed,
Pain at her side, and Megrim at her head.
Two handmaids wait the throne: alike in place,
But diff'ring far in figure and in face.
Here stood Ill-nature like an ancient maid,
Her wrinkled form in black and white array'd;
With store of pray'rs, for mornings, nights, and noons,
Her hand is fill'd; her bosom with lampoons.
There Affectation with a sickly mien,
Shows in her cheek the roses of eighteen,
Practis'd to lisp, and hang the head aside,
Faints into airs, and languishes with pride,
On the rich quilt sinks with becoming woe,
Wrapt in a gown, for sickness, and for show.
The fair-ones feel such maladies as these,
When each new night-dress gives a new disease.
A constant Vapour o'er the palace flies;
Strange phantoms rising as the mists arise;
Dreadful, as hermit's dreams in haunted shades,
Or bright, as visions of expiring maids.

Now glaring fiends, and snakes on rolling spires,
Pale spectres, gaping tombs, and purple fires:
Now lakes of liquid gold, Elysian scenes,
And crystal domes, and Angels in machines.
  Unnumber'd throngs on ev'ry side are seen,
Of bodies chang'd to various forms by Spleen.
Here living Tea-pots stand, one arm held out,
One bent; the handle this, and that the spout:
A Pipkin there, like Homer's Tripod walks;
Here sighs a Jar, and there a Goose-pye talks;
Men prove with child, as pow'rful fancy works,
And maids, turn'd bottles, call aloud for corks.
  Safe past the Gnome thro' this fantastic band,
A branch of healing Spleenwort in his hand.
Then thus address'd the pow'r—Hail wayward Queen!
Who rule the sex to fifty from fifteen:
Parent of vapours and of female wit,
Who give th' hysteric, or poetic fit,
On various tempers act by various ways,
Make some take physic, others scribble plays;
Who cause the proud their visits to delay,
And send the godly in a pet to pray.
A nymph there is, that all thy pow'r disdains,
And thousands more in equal mirth maintains.
But oh! if e'er thy Gnome could spoil a grace,
Or raise a pimple on a beauteous face,
Like Citron-waters matrons' cheeks inflame,
Or change complexions at a losing game;
If e'er with airy horns I planted heads,
Or rumpled petticoats, or tumbled beds,
Or caus'd suspicion when no soul was rude,
Or discompos'd the head-dress of a Prude,
Or e'er to costive lap-dog gave disease,
Which not the tears of brightest eyes could ease:

Hear me, and touch Belinda with chagrin,
That single act gives half the world the spleen.
  The Goddess with a discontented air
Seems to reject him, tho' she grants his pray'r.
A wond'rous Bag with both her hands she binds,
Like that where once Ulysses held the winds;
There she collects the force of female lungs,
Sighs, sobs, and passions, and the war of tongues.
A Vial next she fills with fainting fears,
Soft sorrows, melting griefs, and flowing tears.
The Gnome rejoicing bears her gifts away,
Spreads his black wings, and slowly mounts to day.
  Sunk in Thalestris' arms the nymph he found,
Her eyes dejected and her hair unbound.
Full o'er their heads the swelling bag he rent,
And all the Furies issu'd at the vent.
Belinda burns with more than mortal ire,
And fierce Thalestris fans the rising fire.
O wretched maid! she spread her hands, and cry'd,
(While Hampton's echoes, wretched maid! reply'd)
Was it for this you took such constant care
The bodkin, comb, and essence to prepare?
For this your locks in paper durance bound,
For this with tort'ring irons wreath'd around?
For this with fillets strain'd your tender head,
And bravely bore the double loads of lead?
Gods! shall the ravisher display your hair,
While the Fops envy, and the Ladies stare!
Honour forbid! at whose unrival'd shrine
Ease, pleasure, virtue, all our sex resign.
Methinks already I your tears survey,
Already hear the horrid things they say,
Already see you a degraded toast,
And all your honour in a whisper lost!

How shall I, then, your helpless fame defend?
'Twill then be infamy to seem your friend!
And shall this prize, th' inestimable prize,
Expos'd thro' crystal to the gazing eyes,
And heighten'd by the diamond's circling rays,
On that rapacious hand for ever blaze?
Sooner shall grass in Hyde-park Circus grow,
And wits take lodgings in the sound of Bow;
Sooner let earth, air, sea, to Chaos fall,
Men, monkeys, lap-dogs, parrots, perish all!
She said; then raging to Sir Plume repairs,
And bids her Beau demand the precious hairs:
(Sir Plume of amber snuff-box justly vain,
And the nice conduct of a clouded cane)
With earnest eyes, and round unthinking face,
He first the snuff-box open'd, then the case,
And thus broke out—'My Lord, why, what the devil?
'Z—ds! damn the lock! 'fore Gad, you must be civil!
'Plague on't! 'tis past a jest—nay prithee, pox!
'Give her the hair'—he spoke, and rapp'd his box.
It grieves me much (reply'd the Peer again)
Who speaks so well should ever speak in vain.
But by this Lock, this sacred Lock I swear,
(Which never more shall join its parted hair;
Which never more its honours shall renew,
Clip'd from the lovely head where late it grew)
That while my nostrils draw the vital air,
This hand, which won it, shall for ever wear.
He spoke, and speaking, in proud triumph spread
The long-contended honours of her head.
But Umbriel, hateful Gnome! forbears not so;
He breaks the Vial whence the sorrows flow.
Then see! the nymph in beauteous grief appears,
Her eyes half-languishing, half-drown'd in tears:

On her heav'd bosom hung her drooping head,
Which, with a sigh, she rais'd; and thus she said.
For ever curs'd be this detested day,
Which snatch'd my best, my fav'rite curl away!
Happy! ah ten times happy had I been,
If Hampton-Court these eyes had never seen!
Yet am not I the first mistaken maid,
By love of Courts to num'rous ills betray'd.
Oh had I rather un-admir'd remain'd
In some lone isle, or distant Northern land;
Where the gilt Chariot never marks the way,
Where none learn Ombre, none e'er taste Bohea!
There kept my charms conceal'd from mortal eye,
Like roses, that in deserts bloom and die.
What mov'd my mind with youthful Lords to roam?
O had I stay'd, and said my pray'rs at home!
'Twas this, the morning omens seem'd to tell,
Thrice from my trembling hand the patch-box fell;
The tott'ring China shook without a wind,
Nay Poll sat mute, and Shock was most unkind!
A Sylph too warn'd me of the threats of fate,
In mystic visions, now believ'd too late!
See the poor remnants of these slighted hairs!
My hands shall rend what ev'n thy rapine spares:
These in two sable ringlets taught to break,
Once gave new beauties to the snowy neck;
The sister-lock now sits uncouth, alone,
And in its fellow's fate foresees its own;
Uncurl'd it hangs, the fatal sheers demands,
And tempts, once more, thy sacrilegious hands.
Oh hadst thou, cruel! been content to seize
Hairs less in sight, or any hairs but these!

CANTO V

She said: the pitying audience melt in tears.
But Fate and Jove had stopp'd the Baron's ears.
In vain Thalestris with reproach assails,
For who can move when fair Belinda fails?
Not half so fix'd the Trojan could remain,
While Anna begg'd and Dido rag'd in vain.
Then grave Clarissa graceful wav'd her fan;
Silence ensu'd, and thus the nymph began.
Say why are Beauties prais'd and honour'd most,
The wise man's passion, and the vain man's toast?
Why deck'd with all that land and sea afford,
Why Angels call'd, and Angel-like ador'd?
Why round our coaches croud the white-glov'd Beaux,
Why bows the side-box from its inmost rows?
How vain are all these glories, all our pains,
Unless good sense preserve what beauty gains:
That men may say, when we the front-box grace,
Behold the first in virtue as in face!
Oh! if to dance all night, and dress all day,
Charm'd the small-pox, or chas'd old-age away;
Who would not scorn what housewife's cares produce,
Or who would learn one earthly thing of use?
To patch, nay ogle, might become a Saint,
Nor could it sure be such a sin to paint.
But since, alas! frail beauty must decay,
Curl'd or uncurl'd, since Locks will turn to grey;
Since painted, or not painted, all shall fade,
And she who scorns a man, must die a maid;
What then remains but well our pow'r to use,
And keep good-humour still whate'er we lose?
And trust me, dear! good-humour can prevail,
When airs, and flights, and screams, and scolding fail.

Beauties in vain their pretty eyes may roll;
Charms strike the sight, but merit wins the soul.
  So spoke the Dame, but no applause ensu'd;
Belinda frown'd, Thalestris call'd her Prude.
To arms, to arms! the fierce Virago cries,
And swift as lightning to the combat flies.
All side in parties, and begin th' attack;
Fans clap, silks russle, and tough whalebones crack;
Heroes and Heroines shouts confus'dly rise,
And base, and treble voices strike the skies.
No common weapons in their hands are found,
Like Gods they fight, nor dread a mortal wound.
  So when bold Homer makes the Gods engage,
And heav'nly breasts with human passions rage;
'Gainst Pallas, Mars; Latona, Hermes arms;
And all Olympus rings with loud alarms:
Jove's thunder roars, heav'n trembles all around,
Blue Neptune storms, the bellowing deeps resound:
Earth shakes her nodding towr's, the ground gives way,
And the pale ghosts start at the flash of day!
  Triumphant Umbriel on a sconce's height
Clap'd his glad wings, and sate to view the fight:
Prop'd on their bodkin spears, the Sprites survey
The growing combat, or assist the fray.
  While thro' the press enrag'd Thalestris flies,
And scatters death around from both her eyes,
A Beau and Witling perish'd in the throng,
One dy'd in metaphor, and one in song.
'O cruel nymph! a living death I bear,'
Cry'd Dapperwit, and sunk beside his chair.
A mournful glance Sir Fopling upwards cast,
'Those eyes are made so killing'—was his last.
Thus on Mæander's flow'ry margin lies
Th' expiring Swan, and as he sings he dies.

When bold Sir Plume had drawn Clarissa down,
Chloe stepp'd in, and kill'd him with a frown;
She smil'd to see the doughty hero slain,
But, at her smile, the Beau reviv'd again.
Now Jove suspends his golden scales in air,
Weighs the Men's wits against the Lady's hair;
The doubtful beam long nods from side to side;
At length the wits mount up, the hairs subside.
See fierce Belinda on the Baron flies,
With more than usual lightning in her eyes:
Nor fear'd the Chief th' unequal fight to try,
Who sought no more than on his foe to die.
But this bold Lord with manly strength endu'd,
She with one finger and a thumb subdu'd:
Just where the breath of life his nostrils drew,
A charge of Snuff the wily virgin threw;
The Gnomes direct, to ev'ry atom just,
The pungent grains of titillating dust.
Sudden, with starting tears each eye o'erflows,
And the high dome re-echoes to his nose.
Now meet thy fate, incens'd Belinda cry'd,
And drew a deadly bodkin from her side.
(The same, his ancient personage to deck,
Her great grandsire wore about his neck,
In three seal-rings; which after, melted down,
Form'd a vast buckle for his widow's gown:
Her infant grandame's whistle next it grew,
The bells she jingled, and the whistle blew;
Then in a bodkin grac'd her mother's hairs,
Which long she wore, and now Belinda wears.)
Boast not my fall (he cry'd) insulting foe!
Thou by some other shalt be laid as low.
Nor think, to die dejects my lofty mind:
All that I dread is leaving you behind!

Rather than so, ah let me still survive,
And burn in Cupid's flames,—but burn alive.
  Restore the Lock! she cries; and all around
Restore the Lock! the vaulted roofs rebound.
Not fierce Othello in so loud a strain
Roar'd for the handkerchief that caus'd his pain.
But see how oft ambitious aims are cross'd,
And chiefs contend 'till all the prize is lost!
The Lock, obtain'd with guilt, and kept with pain,
In ev'ry place is sought, but sought in vain:
With such a prize no mortal must be blest,
So heav'n decrees! with heav'n who can contest?
  Some thought it mounted to the Lunar sphere,
Since all things lost on earth are treasur'd there.
There Hero's wits are kept in pond'rous vases,
And Beau's in snuff-boxes and tweezer-cases.
There broken vows, and death-bed alms are found,
And lovers hearts with ends of ribband bound,
The courtier's promises, and sick man's pray'rs,
The smiles of harlots, and the tears of heirs,
Cages for gnats, and chains to yoak a flea,
Dry'd butterflies, and tomes of casuistry.
  But trust the Muse—she saw it upward rise,
Tho' mark'd by none but quick, poetic eyes:
(So Rome's great founder to the heav'ns withdrew,
To Proculus alone confess'd in view)
A sudden Star, it shot thro' liquid air,
And drew behind a radiant trail of hair.
Not Berenice's Locks first rose so bright,
The heav'ns bespangling with dishevel'd light.
The Sylphs behold it kindling as it flies,
And pleas'd pursue its progress thro' the skies.
  This the Beau monde shall from the Mall survey,
And hail with music its propitious ray.

This the blest Lover shall for Venus take,
And send up vows from Rosamonda's lake.
This Partridge soon shall view in cloudless skies,
When next he looks thro' Galilæo's eyes;
And hence th' egregious wizard shall foredoom
The fate of Louis, and the fall of Rome.
Then cease, bright Nymph! to mourn thy ravish'd hair,
Which adds new glory to the shining sphere!
Not all the tresses that fair head can boast,
Shall draw such envy as the Lock you lost.
For, after all the murders of your eye,
When, after millions slain, yourself shall die;
When those fair suns shall set, as set they must,
And all those tresses shall be laid in dust,
This Lock, the Muse shall consecrate to fame,
And 'midst the stars inscribe Belinda's name.

The Iliad of Homer

Translation published 1715–20

Hector and Andromache

Book VI (1716), lines 544–637

YET while my *Hector* still survives, I see
My Father, Mother, Brethren, all, in thee.
Alas! my Parents, Brothers, Kindred, all,
Once more will perish if my *Hector* fall.
Thy Wife, thy Infant, in thy Danger share:
Oh prove a Husband's and a Father's Care!
That Quarter most the skillful *Greeks* annoy,
Where yon' wild Fig-Trees join the Wall of *Troy*:

Thou, from this Tow'r defend th' important Post;
There *Agamemnon* points his dreadful Host,
That Pass *Tydides*, *Ajax* strive to gain,
And there the vengeful *Spartan* fires his Train.
Thrice our bold Foes the fierce Attack have giv'n,
Or led by Hopes, or dictated from Heav'n.
Let others in the Field their Arms employ,
But stay my *Hector* here, and guard his *Troy*.
The Chief reply'd: That Post shall be my Care,
Nor that alone, but all the Works of War.
How would the Sons of *Troy*, in Arms renown'd,
And *Troy*'s proud Dames whose Garments sweep the Ground,
Attaint the Lustre of my former Name,
Should *Hector* basely quit the Field of Fame?
My early Youth was bred to martial Pains,
My Soul impells me to th' embattel'd Plains;
Let me be foremost to defend the Throne,
And guard my Father's Glories, and my own.
Yet come it will, the Day decreed by Fates;
(How my Heart trembles while my Tongue relates!)
The Day when thou, Imperial *Troy!* must bend,
And see thy Warriors fall, thy Glories end.
And yet no dire Presage so wounds my Mind,
My Mother's Death, the Ruin of my Kind,
Not *Priam*'s hoary Hairs defil'd with Gore,
Not all my Brothers gasping on the Shore;
As thine, *Andromache!* thy Griefs I dread;
I see thee trembling, weeping, Captive led!
In *Argive* Looms our Battels to design,
And Woes, of which so large a Part was thine!
To bear the Victor's hard Commands, or bring
The Weight of Waters from *Hyperia*'s Spring.
There, while you groan beneath the Load of Life,
They cry, Behold the mighty *Hector*'s Wife!

Some haughty *Greek* who lives thy Tears to see,
Embitters all thy Woes, by naming me.
The Thoughts of Glory past, and present Shame,
A thousand Griefs shall waken at the Name!
May I lie cold before that dreadful Day,
Press'd with a Load of Monumental Clay!
Thy *Hector* wrapt in everlasting Sleep,
Shall neither hear thee sigh, nor see thee weep.
  Thus having spoke, th' illustrious Chief of *Troy*
Stretch'd his fond Arms to clasp the lovely Boy.
The Babe clung crying to his Nurse's Breast,
Scar'd at the dazling Helm, and nodding Crest.
With secret Pleasure each fond Parent smil'd,
And *Hector* hasted to relieve his Child,
The glitt'ring Terrors from his Brows unbound,
And plac'd the beaming Helmet on the Ground.
Then kist the Child, and lifting high in Air,
Thus to the Gods prefer'd a Father's Pray'r.
  O Thou! whose Glory fills th' Ætherial Throne,
And all ye deathless Pow'rs! protect my Son!
Grant him, like me, to purchase just Renown,
To guard the *Trojans*, to defend the Crown,
Against his Country's Foes the War to wage,
And rise the *Hector* of the future Age!
So when triumphant from successful Toils,
Of Heroes slain he bears the reeking Spoils,
Whole Hosts may hail him with deserv'd Acclaim,
And say, This Chief transcends his Father's Fame:
While pleas'd amidst the gen'ral Shouts of *Troy*,
His Mother's conscious Heart o'erflows with Joy.
  He spoke, and fondly gazing on her Charms
Restor'd the pleasing Burden to her Arms;
Soft on her fragrant Breast the Babe she laid,
Hush'd to Repose, and with a Smile survey'd.

The troubled Pleasure soon chastis'd by Fear,
She mingled with the Smile a tender Tear.
The soften'd Chief with kind Compassion view'd,
And dry'd the falling Drops, and thus pursu'd.
Andromache! my Soul's far better Part,
Why with untimely Sorrows heaves thy Heart?
No hostile Hand can antedate my Doom,
Till Fate condemns me to the silent Tomb.
Fix'd is the Term to all the Race of Earth,
And such the hard Condition of our Birth.
No Force can then resist, no Flight can save,
All sink alike, the Fearful and the Brave.
No more—but hasten to thy Tasks at home,
There guide the Spindle, and direct the Loom:
Me Glory summons to the Martial Scene,
The Field of Combat is the Sphere for Men.
Where Heroes war, the foremost Place I claim,
The first in Danger as the first in Fame.

To a Young LADY
On her leaving the Town after
the Coronation

The Works of Mr. Alexander Pope, 1717

As some fond virgin, whom her mother's care
Drags from the town to wholesome country air,
Just when she learns to roll a melting eye,
And hear a spark, yet think no danger nigh;
From the dear man unwilling she must sever,
Yet takes one kiss before she parts for ever:

Thus from the world fair Zephalinda flew,
Saw others happy, and with sighs withdrew;
Not that their pleasures caus'd her discontent,
She sigh'd not that They stay'd, but that She went.
  She went, to plain-work and to purling brooks,
Old-fashion'd halls, dull aunts, and croaking rooks:
She went from Op'ra, Park, Assembly, Play,
To morning walks, and pray'rs three hours a day;
To part her time 'twixt reading and bohea,
To muse, and spill her solitary tea,
Or o'er cold coffee trifle with the spoon,
Count the slow clock, and dine exact at noon;
Divert her eyes with pictures in the fire,
Hum half a tune, tell stories to the squire;
Up to her godly garret after sev'n,
There starve and pray, for that 's the way to heav'n.
  Some Squire, perhaps, you take delight to rack;
Whose game is Whisk, whose treat a toast in sack;
Who visits with a gun, presents you birds,
Then gives a smacking buss, and cries,—No words!
Or with his hound comes hollowing from the stable,
Makes love with nods, and knees beneath a table;
Whose laughs are hearty, tho' his jests are coarse,
And loves you best of all things—but his horse.
  In some fair evening, on your elbow laid,
You dream of triumphs in the rural shade;
In pensive thought recall the fancy'd scene,
See Coronations rise on ev'ry green;
Before you pass th' imaginary sights
Of Lords, and Earls, and Dukes, and garter'd Knights,
While the spread fan o'ershades your closing eyes;
Then give one flirt, and all the vision flies.
Thus vanish sceptres, coronets, and balls,
And leave you in lone woods, or empty walls.

So when your Slave, at some dear, idle time,
(Not plagu'd with head-achs, or the want of rhyme)
Stands in the streets, abstracted from the crew,
And while he seems to study, thinks of you;
Just when his fancy points your sprightly eyes,
Or sees the blush of Parthenissa rise,
Gay pats my shoulder, and you vanish quite,
Streets, chairs, and coxcombs rush upon my sight;
Vex'd to be still in town, I knit my brow,
Look sour, and hum a song—as you may now.

Elegy to the Memory of an UNFORTUNATE LADY

The Works of Mr. Alexander Pope, 1717

WHAT beck'ning ghost, along the moonlight shade
Invites my steps, and points to yonder glade?
'Tis she!—but why that bleeding bosom gor'd,
Why dimly gleams the visionary sword?
Oh ever beauteous, ever friendly! tell,
Is it, in heav'n, a crime to love too well?
To bear too tender, or too firm a heart,
To act a Lover's or a Roman's part?
Is there no bright reversion in the sky,
For those who greatly think, or bravely die?
Why bade ye else, ye Pow'rs! her soul aspire
Above the vulgar flight of low desire?
Ambition first sprung from your blest abodes;
The glorious fault of Angels and of Gods:
Thence to their images on earth it flows,
And in the breasts of Kings and Heroes glows.

Most souls, 'tis true, but peep out once an age,
Dull sullen pris'ners in the body's cage:
Dim lights of life, that burn a length of years
Useless, unseen, as lamps in sepulchres;
Like Eastern Kings a lazy state they keep,
And close confin'd to their own palace, sleep.
  From these perhaps (ere nature bade her die)
Fate snatch'd her early to the pitying sky.
As into air the purer spirits flow,
And sep'rate from their kindred dregs below;
So flew the soul to its congenial place,
Nor left one virtue to redeem her Race.
  But thou, false guardian of a charge too good,
Thou, mean deserter of thy brother's blood!
See on these ruby lips the trembling breath,
These cheeks, now fading at the blast of death;
Cold is that breast which warm'd the world before,
And those love-darting eyes must roll no more.
Thus, if Eternal justice rules the ball,
Thus shall your wives, and thus your children fall:
On all the line a sudden vengeance waits,
And frequent herses shall besiege your gates.
There passengers shall stand, and pointing say,
(While the long fun'rals blacken all the way)
Lo these were they, whose souls the Furies steel'd,
And curs'd with hearts unknowing how to yield.
Thus unlamented pass the proud away,
The gaze of fools, and pageant of a day!
So perish all, whose breast ne'er learn'd to glow
For others good, or melt at others woe.
  What can atone (oh ever-injur'd shade!)
Thy fate unpity'd, and thy rites unpaid?
No friend's complaint, no kind domestic tear
Pleas'd thy pale ghost, or grac'd thy mournful bier.

By foreign hands thy dying eyes were clos'd,
By foreign hands thy decent limbs compos'd,
By foreign hands thy humble grave adorn'd,
By strangers honour'd, and by strangers mourn'd!
What tho' no friends in sable weeds appear,
Grieve for an hour, perhaps, then mourn a year,
And bear about the mockery of woe
To midnight dances, and the public show?
What tho' no weeping Loves thy ashes grace,
Nor polish'd marble emulate thy face?
What tho' no sacred earth allow thee room,
Nor hallow'd dirge be mutter'd o'er thy tomb?
Yet shall thy grave with rising flow'rs be drest,
And the green turf lie lightly on thy breast:
There shall the morn her earliest tears bestow,
There the first roses of the year shall blow;
While Angels with their silver wings o'ershade
The ground, now sacred by thy reliques made.
  So peaceful rests, without a stone, a name,
What once had beauty, titles, wealth, and fame.
How lov'd, how honour'd once, avails thee not,
To whom related, or by whom begot;
A heap of dust alone remains of thee,
'Tis all thou art, and all the proud shall be!
  Poets themselves must fall, like those they sung,
Deaf the prais'd ear, and mute the tuneful tongue.
Ev'n he, whose soul now melts in mournful lays,
Shall shortly want the gen'rous tear he pays;
Then from his closing eyes thy form shall part,
And the last pang shall tear thee from his heart,
Life's idle business at one gasp be o'er,
The Muse forgot, and thou belov'd no more!

ELOISA to ABELARD

The Works of Mr. Alexander Pope, 1717

In these deep solitudes and awful cells,
Where heav'nly-pensive contemplation dwells,
And ever-musing melancholy reigns;
What means this tumult in a Vestal's veins?
Why rove my thoughts beyond this last retreat?
Why feels my heart its long-forgotten heat?
Yet, yet I love!—From Abelard it came,
And Eloïsa yet must kiss the name.
Dear fatal name! rest ever unreveal'd,
Nor pass these lips in holy silence seal'd:
Hide it, my heart, within that close disguise,
Where mix'd with God's, his lov'd Idea lies:
O write it not my hand—the name appears
Already written—wash it out, my tears!
In vain lost Eloïsa weeps and prays,
Her heart still dictates, and her hand obeys.
Relentless walls! whose darksome round contains
Repentant sighs, and voluntary pains:
Ye rugged rocks! which holy knees have worn;
Ye grots and caverns shagg'd with horrid thorn!
Shrines! where their vigils pale-ey'd virgins keep,
And pitying saints, whose statues learn to weep!
Tho' cold like you, unmov'd and silent grown,
I have not yet forgot myself to stone.
All is not Heav'n's while Abelard has part,
Still rebel nature holds out half my heart;
Nor pray'rs nor fasts its stubborn pulse restrain,
Nor tears for ages taught to flow in vain.
Soon as thy letters trembling I unclose,
That well-known name awakens all my woes.

Oh name for ever sad! for ever dear!
Still breath'd in sighs, still usher'd with a tear.
I tremble too, where'er my own I find,
Some dire misfortune follows close behind.
Line after line my gushing eyes o'erflow,
Led thro' a sad variety of woe:
Now warm in love, now with'ring in my bloom,
Lost in a convent's solitary gloom!
There stern Religion quench'd th' unwilling flame,
There dy'd the best of passions, Love and Fame.
  Yet write, oh write me all, that I may join
Griefs to thy griefs, and echo sighs to thine.
Nor foes nor fortune take this pow'r away;
And is my Abelard less kind than they?
Tears still are mine, and those I need not spare,
Love but demands what else were shed in pray'r;
No happier task these faded eyes pursue;
To read and weep is all they now can do.
  Then share thy pain, allow that sad relief;
Ah, more than share it, give me all thy grief.
Heav'n first taught letters for some wretch's aid,
Some banish'd lover, or some captive maid;
They live, they speak, they breathe what love inspires,
Warm from the soul, and faithful to its fires,
The virgin's wish without her fears impart,
Excuse the blush, and pour out all the heart,
Speed the soft intercourse from soul to soul,
And waft a sigh from Indus to the Pole.
  Thou know'st how guiltless first I met thy flame,
When Love approach'd me under Friendship's name;
My fancy form'd thee of angelic kind,
Some emanation of th' all-beauteous Mind.
Those smiling eyes, attemp'ring ev'ry ray,
Shone sweetly lambent with celestial day.

Guiltless I gaz'd; heav'n listen'd while you sung;
And truths divine came mended from that tongue.
From lips like those what precept fail'd to move?
Too soon they taught me 'twas no sin to love:
Back thro' the paths of pleasing sense I ran,
Nor wish'd an Angel whom I lov'd a Man.
Dim and remote the joys of saints I see;
Nor envy them that heav'n I lose for thee.
  How oft, when press'd to marriage, have I said,
Curse on all laws but those which love has made?
Love, free as air, at sight of human ties,
Spreads his light wings, and in a moment flies.
Let wealth, let honour, wait the wedded dame,
August her deed, and sacred be her fame;
Before true passion all those views remove,
Fame, wealth, and honour! what are you to Love?
The jealous God, when we profane his fires,
Those restless passions in revenge inspires,
And bids them make mistaken mortals groan,
Who seek in love for aught but love alone.
Should at my feet the world's great master fall,
Himself, his throne, his world, I'd scorn 'em all:
Not Cæsar's empress would I deign to prove;
No, make me mistress to the man I love;
If there be yet another name more free,
More fond than mistress, make me that to thee!
Oh! happy state! when souls each other draw,
When love is liberty, and nature, law:
All then is full, possessing, and possess'd,
No craving void left aking in the breast:
Ev'n thought meets thought, ere from the lips it part,
And each warm wish springs mutual from the heart.
This sure is bliss (if bliss on earth there be)
And once the lot of Abelard and me.

Alas how chang'd! what sudden horrors rise!
A naked Lover bound and bleeding lies!
Where, where was Eloïse? her voice, her hand,
Her ponyard, had oppos'd the dire command.
Barbarian, stay! that bloody stroke restrain;
The crime was common, common be the pain.
I can no more; by shame, by rage suppress'd,
Let tears, and burning blushes speak the rest.
Canst thou forget that sad, that solemn day,
When victims at yon altar's foot we lay?
Canst thou forget what tears that moment fell,
When, warm in youth, I bade the world farewell?
As with cold lips I kiss'd the sacred veil,
The shrines all trembled, and the lamps grew pale:
Heav'n scarce believ'd the Conquest it survey'd,
And Saints with wonder heard the vows I made.
Yet then, to those dread altars as I drew,
Not on the Cross my eyes were fix'd, but you:
Not grace, or zeal, love only was my call,
And if I lose thy love, I lose my all.
Come! with thy looks, thy words, relieve my woe;
Those still at least are left thee to bestow.
Still on that breast enamour'd let me lie,
Still drink delicious poison from thy eye,
Pant on thy lip, and to thy heart be press'd;
Give all thou canst—and let me dream the rest.
Ah no! instruct me other joys to prize,
With other beauties charm my partial eyes,
Full in my view set all the bright abode,
And make my soul quit Abelard for God.
Ah think at least thy flock deserves thy care,
Plants of thy hand, and children of thy pray'r.
From the false world in early youth they fled,
By thee to mountains, wilds, and deserts led.

You rais'd these hallow'd walls; the desert smil'd,
And Paradise was open'd in the Wild.
No weeping orphan saw his father's stores
Our shrines irradiate, or emblaze the floors;
No silver saints, by dying misers giv'n,
Here brib'd the rage of ill-requited heav'n:
But such plain roofs as Piety could raise,
And only vocal with the Maker's praise.
In these lone walls (their days eternal bound)
These moss-grown domes with spiry turrets crown'd,
Where awful arches make a noon-day night,
And the dim windows shed a solemn light;
Thy eyes diffus'd a reconciling ray,
And gleams of glory brighten'd all the day.
But now no face divine contentment wears,
'Tis all blank sadness, or continual tears.
See how the force of others pray'rs I try,
(O pious fraud of am'rous charity!)
But why should I on others pray'rs depend?
Come thou, my father, brother, husband, friend!
Ah let thy handmaid, sister, daughter move,
And all those tender names in one, thy love!
The darksome pines that o'er yon rocks reclin'd
Wave high, and murmur to the hollow wind,
The wand'ring streams that shine between the hills,
The grots that echo to the tinkling rills,
The dying gales that pant upon the trees,
The lakes that quiver to the curling breeze;
No more these scenes my meditation aid,
Or lull to rest the visionary maid.
But o'er the twilight groves and dusky caves,
Long-sounding isles, and intermingled graves,
Black Melancholy sits, and round her throws
A death-like silence, and a dread repose:

Her gloomy presence saddens all the scene,
Shades ev'ry flow'r, and darkens ev'ry green,
Deepens the murmur of the falling floods,
And breathes a browner horror on the woods.
  Yet here for ever, ever must I stay;
Sad proof how well a lover can obey!
Death, only death, can break the lasting chain;
And here, ev'n then, shall my cold dust remain,
Here all its frailties, all its flames resign,
And wait till 'tis no sin to mix with thine.
  Ah wretch! believ'd the spouse of God in vain,
Confess'd within the slave of love and man.
Assist me, heav'n! but whence arose that pray'r?
Sprung it from piety, or from despair?
Ev'n here, where frozen chastity retires,
Love finds an altar for forbidden fires.
I ought to grieve, but cannot what I ought;
I mourn the lover, not lament the fault;
I view my crime, but kindle at the view,
Repent old pleasures, and solicit new;
Now turn'd to heav'n, I weep my past offence,
Now think of thee, and curse my innocence.
Of all affliction taught a lover yet,
'Tis sure the hardest science to forget!
How shall I lose the sin, yet keep the sense,
And love th' offender, yet detest th' offence?
How the dear object from the crime remove,
Or how distinguish penitence from love?
Unequal task! a passion to resign,
For hearts so touch'd, so pierc'd, so lost as mine.
Ere such a soul regains its peaceful state,
How often must it love, how often hate!
How often hope, despair, resent, regret,
Conceal, disdain,—do all things but forget.

But let heav'n seize it, all at once 'tis fir'd;
Not touch'd, but rapt; not waken'd, but inspir'd!
Oh come! oh teach me nature to subdue,
Renounce my love, my life, my self—and you.
Fill my fond heart with God alone, for he
Alone can rival, can succeed to thee.
  How happy is the blameless Vestal's lot?
The world forgetting, by the world forgot:
Eternal sun-shine of the spotless mind!
Each pray'r accepted, and each wish resign'd;
Labour and rest, that equal periods keep;
'Obedient slumbers that can wake and weep;'
Desires compos'd, affections ever ev'n;
Tears that delight, and sighs that waft to heav'n.
Grace shines around her with serenest beams,
And whisp'ring Angels prompt her golden dreams.
For her th' unfading rose of Eden blooms,
And wings of Seraphs shed divine perfumes,
For her the Spouse prepares the bridal ring,
For her white virgins Hymenæals sing,
To sounds of heav'nly harps she dies away,
And melts in visions of eternal day.
  Far other dreams my erring soul employ,
Far other raptures, of unholy joy:
When at the close of each sad, sorrowing day,
Fancy restores what vengeance snatch'd away,
Then conscience sleeps, and leaving nature free,
All my loose soul unbounded springs to thee.
O curst, dear horrors of all-conscious night!
How glowing guilt exalts the keen delight!
Provoking Dæmons all restraint remove,
And stir within me ev'ry source of love.
I hear thee, view thee, gaze o'er all thy charms,
And round thy phantom glue my clasping arms.

I wake:—no more I hear, no more I view,
The phantom flies me, as unkind as you.
I call aloud; it hears not what I say:
I stretch my empty arms; it glides away.
To dream once more I close my willing eyes;
Ye soft illusions, dear deceits, arise!
Alas, no more! methinks we wand'ring go
Thro' dreary wastes, and weep each other's woe,
Where round some mould'ring tow'r pale ivy creeps,
And low-brow'd rocks hang nodding o'er the deeps.
Sudden you mount, you beckon from the skies;
Clouds interpose, waves roar, and winds arise.
I shriek, start up, the same sad prospect find,
And wake to all the griefs I left behind.
  For thee the fates, severely kind, ordain
A cool suspense from pleasure and from pain;
Thy life a long dead calm of fix'd repose;
No pulse that riots, and no blood that glows.
Still as the sea, ere winds were taught to blow,
Or moving spirit bade the waters flow;
Soft as the slumbers of a saint forgiv'n,
And mild as op'ning gleams of promis'd heav'n.
  Come, Abelard! for what hast thou to dread?
The torch of Venus burns not for the dead.
Nature stands check'd; Religion disapproves;
Ev'n thou art cold—yet Eloïsa loves.
Ah hopeless, lasting flames! like those that burn
To light the dead, and warm th' unfruitful urn.
  What scenes appear where'er I turn my view?
The dear Ideas, where I fly, pursue,
Rise in the grove, before the altar rise,
Stain all my soul, and wanton in my eyes.
I waste the Matin lamp in sighs for thee,
Thy image steals between my God and me,

Thy voice I seem in ev'ry hymn to hear,
With ev'ry bead I drop too soft a tear.
When from the censer clouds of fragrance roll,
And swelling organs lift the rising soul,
One thought of thee puts all the pomp to flight,
Priests, tapers, temples, swim before my sight:
In seas of flame my plunging soul is drown'd,
While Altars blaze, and Angels tremble round.
  While prostrate here in humble grief I lie,
Kind, virtuous drops just gath'ring in my eye,
While praying, trembling, in the dust I roll,
And dawning grace is op'ning on my soul:
Come, if thou dar'st, all charming as thou art!
Oppose thyself to heav'n; dispute my heart;
Come, with one glance of those deluding eyes
Blot out each bright Idea of the skies;
Take back that grace, those sorrows, and those tears;
Take back my fruitless penitence and pray'rs;
Snatch me, just mounting, from the blest abode;
Assist the fiends, and tear me from my God!
  No, fly me, fly me, far as Pole from Pole;
Rise Alps between us! and whole oceans roll!
Ah, come not, write not, think not once of me,
Nor share one pang of all I felt for thee.
Thy oaths I quit, thy memory resign;
Forget, renounce me, hate whate'er was mine.
Fair eyes, and tempting looks (which yet I view!)
Long lov'd, ador'd ideas, all adieu!
O Grace serene! oh virtue heav'nly fair!
Divine oblivion of low-thoughted care!
Fresh blooming Hope, gay daughter of the sky!
And Faith, our early immortality!
Enter, each mild, each amicable guest;
Receive, and wrap me in eternal rest!

See in her cell sad Eloïsa spread,
Propt on some tomb, a neighbour of the dead.
In each low wind methinks a Spirit calls,
And more than Echoes talk along the walls.
Here, as I watch'd the dying lamps around,
From yonder shrine I heard a hollow sound.
'Come, sister, come! (it said, or seem'd to say)
'Thy place is here, sad sister, come away!
'Once like thyself, I trembled, wept, and pray'd,
'Love's victim then, tho' now a sainted maid:
'But all is calm in this eternal sleep;
'Here grief forgets to groan, and love to weep,
'Ev'n superstition loses ev'ry fear:
'For God, not man, absolves our frailties here.'

I come, I come! prepare your roseate bow'rs,
Celestial palms, and ever-blooming flow'rs.
Thither, where sinners may have rest, I go,
Where flames refin'd in breasts seraphic glow:
Thou, Abelard! the last sad office pay,
And smooth my passage to the realms of day;
See my lips tremble, and my eye-balls roll,
Suck my last breath, and catch my flying soul!
Ah no—in sacred vestments may'st thou stand,
The hallow'd taper trembling in thy hand,
Present the Cross before my lifted eye,
Teach me at once, and learn of me to die.
Ah then, thy once-lov'd Eloïsa see!
It will be then no crime to gaze on me.
See from my cheek the transient roses fly!
See the last sparkle languish in my eye!
'Till ev'ry motion, pulse, and breath be o'er;
And ev'n my Abelard be lov'd no more.
O Death all-eloquent! you only prove
What dust we doat on, when 'tis man we love.

Then too, when fate shall thy fair frame destroy,
(That cause of all my guilt, and all my joy)
In trance extatic may thy pangs be drown'd,
Bright clouds descend, and Angels watch thee round,
From op'ning skies may streaming glories shine,
And Saints embrace thee with a love like mine.
May one kind grave unite each hapless name,
And graft my love immortal on thy fame!
Then, ages hence, when all my woes are o'er,
When this rebellious heart shall beat no more;
If ever chance two wand'ring lovers brings
To Paraclete's white walls and silver springs,
O'er the pale marble shall they join their heads,
And drink the falling tears each other sheds;
Then sadly say, with mutual pity mov'd,
'Oh may we never love as these have lov'd!'
From the full choir when loud Hosannas rise,
And swell the pomp of dreadful sacrifice,
Amid that scene if some relenting eye
Glance on the stone where our cold relicks lie,
Devotion's self shall steal a thought from heav'n,
One human tear shall drop, and be forgiv'n.
And sure if fate some future bard shall join
In sad similitude of griefs to mine,
Condemn'd whole years in absence to deplore,
And image charms he must behold no more;
Such if there be, who loves so long, so well;
Let him our sad, our tender story tell;
The well-sung woes will sooth my pensive ghost;
He best can paint 'em who shall feel 'em most.

Epistle to

Robert, Earl of Oxford

and Earl Mortimer

The Dedication of *Poems on Several Occasions*
Written by Dr. Thomas Parnell, 1722

SUCH were the notes thy once-lov'd Poet sung,
'Till Death untimely stop'd his tuneful tongue.
Oh just beheld, and lost! admir'd and mourn'd!
With softest manners, gentlest arts adorn'd!
Blest in each science, blest in ev'ry strain!
Dear to the Muse! to HARLEY dear—in vain!
For him, thou oft hast bid the World attend,
Fond to forget the statesman in the friend;
For SWIFT and him, despis'd the farce of state,
The sober follies of the wise and great;
Dextrous, the craving, fawning croud to quit,
And pleas'd to 'scape from Flattery to Wit.
Absent or dead, still let a friend be dear,
(A sigh the absent claims, the dead a tear)
Recall those nights that clos'd thy toilsome days,
Still hear thy Parnell in his living lays,
Who, careless now of Int'rest, Fame, or Fate,
Perhaps forgets that OXFORD e'er was great;
Or deeming meanest what we greatest call,
Beholds thee glorious only in thy Fall.
And sure, if aught below the seats divine
Can touch Immortals, 'tis a Soul like thine:
A Soul supreme, in each hard instance try'd,
Above all Pain, all Passion, and all Pride,
The rage of Pow'r, the blast of public breath,
The lust of Lucre, and the dread of Death.

In vain to Deserts thy retreat is made;
The Muse attends thee to thy silent shade:
'Tis hers, the brave man's latest steps to trace,
Rejudge his acts, and dignify disgrace.
When Int'rest calls off all her sneaking train,
And all th' oblig'd desert, and all the vain;
She waits, or to the scaffold, or the cell,
When the last ling'ring friend has bid farewell.
Ev'n now, she shades thy Ev'ning-walk with bays,
(No hireling she, no prostitute to praise)
Ev'n now, observant of the parting ray,
Eyes the calm Sun-set of thy various Day,
Thro' Fortune's cloud one truly great can see,
Nor fears to tell, that MORTIMER is he.

The Odyssey of Homer

Translation published 1725–1726

Ulysses and his Dog

Book XVII (1726), lines 344–99

THUS, near the gates conferring as they drew,
Argus, the Dog, his antient master knew;
He, not unconscious of the voice, and tread,
Lifts to the sound his ear, and rears his head.
Bred by *Ulysses*, nourish'd at his board,
But ah! not fated long to please his Lord!
To him, his swiftness and his strength were vain;
The voice of Glory call'd him o'er the main.
'Till then in ev'ry sylvan chace renown'd,
With *Argus, Argus*, rung the woods around;

With him the youth pursu'd the goat or fawn,
Or trac'd the mazy leveret o'er the lawn.
Now left to man's ingratitude he lay,
Un-hous'd, neglected, in the publick way;
And where on heaps the rich manure was spread,
Obscene with reptiles, took his sordid bed.
He knew his Lord; he knew, and strove to meet,
In vain he strove, to crawl, and kiss his feet;
Yet (all he could) his tail, his ears, his eyes
Salute his master, and confess his joys.
Soft pity touch'd the mighty master's soul;
Adown his cheek a tear unbidden stole,
Stole unperceiv'd; he turn'd his head, and dry'd
The drop humane: then thus impassion'd cry'd.
What noble beast in this abandon'd state
Lies here all helpless at *Ulysses'* gate?
His bulk and beauty speak no vulgar praise;
If, as he seems, he *was* in better days,
Some care his Age deserves: Or was he priz'd
For worthless beauty? therefore now despis'd?
Such dogs, and men there are, meer things of state,
And always cherish'd by their friends, the Great.
Not *Argus* so, (*Eumæus* thus rejoin'd)
But serv'd a master of a nobler kind,
Who never, never shall behold him more!
Long, long since perish'd on a distant shore!
Oh had you seen him, vig'rous, bold and young,
Swift as a stag, and as a lion strong,
Him no fell Savage on the plain withstood,
None 'scap'd him, bosom'd in the gloomy wood;
His eye how piercing, and his scent how true,
To winde the vapour in the tainted dew?
Such, when *Ulysses* left his natal coast;
Now years un-nerve him, and his lord is lost!

The women keep the gen'rous creature bare,
A sleek and idle race is all their care:
The master gone, the servants what restrains?
Or dwells humanity where riot reigns?
Jove fix'd it certain, that whatever day
Makes man a slave, takes half his worth away.
  This said, the honest herdsman strode before:
The musing Monarch pauses at the door:
The Dog whom Fate had granted to behold
His Lord, when twenty tedious years had roll'd,
Takes a last look, and having seen him, dies;
So clos'd for ever faithful *Argus*' eyes!

THE

DUNCIAD,

VARIORVM.

WITH THE

PROLEGOMENA of *SCRIBLERUS.*

DEFEROR IN VICVM

VENDENTEM THVS ET ODORES

LONDON.

Printed for A, DOD. 1729.

The DUNCIAD

1728, 1743

BOOK I

THE Mighty Mother, and her Son, who brings
The Smithfield Muses to the ear of Kings,
I sing. Say you, her instruments the Great!
Call'd to this work by Dulness, Jove, and Fate;
You by whose care, in vain decry'd and curst,
Still Dunce the second reigns like Dunce the first;
Say, how the Goddess bade Britannia sleep,
And pour'd her Spirit o'er the land and deep.
  In eldest time, e'er mortals writ or read,
E'er Pallas issu'd from the Thund'rer's head,
Dulness o'er all possess'd her ancient right,
Daughter of Chaos and eternal Night:
Fate in their dotage this fair Idiot gave,
Gross as her sire, and as her mother grave,
Laborious, heavy, busy, bold, and blind,
She rul'd, in native Anarchy, the mind.
  Still her old Empire to restore she tries,
For, born a Goddess, Dulness never dies.
  O Thou! whatever title please thine ear,
Dean, Drapier, Bickerstaff, or Gulliver!
Whether thou chuse Cervantes' serious air,
Or laugh and shake in Rab'lais' easy chair,
Or praise the Court, or magnify Mankind,
Or thy griev'd Country's copper chains unbind;
From thy Bœotia tho' her Pow'r retires,
Mourn not, my SWIFT, at ought our Realm acquires.
Here pleas'd behold her mighty wings out-spread
To hatch a new Saturnian age of Lead.

Close to those walls where Folly holds her throne,
And laughs to think Monroe would take her down,
Where o'er the gates, by his fam'd father's hand,
Great Cibber's brazen, brainless brothers stand;
One Cell there is, conceal'd from vulgar eye,
The Cave of Poverty and Poetry.
Keen, hollow winds howl thro' the bleak recess,
Emblem of Music caus'd by Emptiness.
Hence Bards, like Proteus long in vain ty'd down,
Escape in Monsters, and amaze the town.
Hence Miscellanies spring, the weekly boast
Of Curl's chaste press, and Lintot's rubric post:
Hence hymning Tyburn's elegiac lines,
Hence Journals, Medley's, Merc'ries, MAGAZINES:
Sepulchral Lies, our holy walls to grace,
And New-year Odes, and all the Grub-street race.
In clouded Majesty here Dulness shone;
Four guardian Virtues, round, support her throne:
Fierce champion Fortitude, that knows no fears
Of hisses, blows, or want, or loss of ears:
Calm Temperance, whose blessings those partake
Who hunger, and who thirst for scribbling sake:
Prudence, whose glass presents th' approaching jayl:
Poetic Justice, with her lifted scale,
Where, in nice balance, truth with gold she weighs,
And solid pudding against empty praise.
Here she beholds the Chaos dark and deep,
Where nameless Somethings in their causes sleep,
'Till genial Jacob, or a warm Third day,
Call forth each mass, a Poem, or a Play:
How hints, like spawn, scarce quick in embryo lie,
How new-born nonsense first is taught to cry,
Maggots half-form'd in rhyme exactly meet,
And learn to crawl upon poetic feet.

Here one poor word an hundred clenches makes,
And ductile dulness new meanders takes;
There motley Images her fancy strike,
Figures ill pair'd, and Similies unlike.
She sees a Mob of Metaphors advance,
Pleas'd with the madness of the mazy dance;
How Tragedy and Comedy embrace;
How Farce and Epic get a jumbled race;
How Time himself stands still at her command,
Realms shift their place, and Ocean turns to land.
Here gay Description Ægypt glads with show'rs,
Or gives to Zembla fruits, to Barca flow'rs;
Glitt'ring with ice here hoary hills are seen,
There painted vallies of eternal green,
In cold December fragrant chaplets blow,
And heavy harvests nod beneath the snow.
  All these, and more, the cloud-compelling Queen
Beholds thro' fogs, that magnify the scene.
She, tinsel'd o'er in robes of varying hues,
With self-applause her wild creation views;
Sees momentary monsters rise and fall,
And with her own fools-colours gilds them all.
  'Twas on the day, when * * rich and grave,
Like Cimon, triumph'd both on land and wave:
(Pomps without guilt, of bloodless swords and maces,
Glad chains, warm furs, broad banners, and broad faces)
Now Night descending, the proud scene was o'er,
But liv'd, in Settle's numbers, one day more.
Now May'rs and Shrieves all hush'd and satiate lay,
Yet eat, in dreams, the custard of the day;
While pensive Poets painful vigils keep,
Sleepless themselves, to give their readers sleep.
Much to the mindful Queen the feast recalls
What City Swans once sung within the walls;

Much she revolves their arts, their ancient praise,
And sure succession down from Heywood's days.
She saw, with joy, the line immortal run,
Each sire imprest and glaring in his son:
So watchful Bruin forms, with plastic care,
Each growing lump, and brings it to a Bear.
She saw old Pryn in restless Daniel shine,
And Eusden eke out Blackmore's endless line;
She saw slow Philips creep like Tate's poor page,
And all the mighty Mad in Dennis rage.
  In each she marks her Image full exprest,
But chief in BAYS's monster-breeding breast;
  Bays, form'd by nature Stage and Town to bless,
And act, and be, a Coxcomb with success.
Dulness with transport eyes the lively Dunce,
Remembring she herself was Pertness once.
Now (shame to Fortune!) an ill Run at Play
Blank'd his bold visage, and a thin Third day:
Swearing and supperless the Hero sate,
Blasphem'd his Gods, the Dice, and damn'd his Fate.
Then gnaw'd his pen, then dash'd it on the ground,
Sinking from thought to thought, a vast profound!
Plung'd for his sense, but found no bottom there,
Yet wrote and flounder'd on, in mere despair.
Round him much Embryo, much Abortion lay,
Much future Ode, and abdicated Play;
Nonsense precipitate, like running Lead,
That slip'd thro' Cracks and Zig-zags of the Head;
All that on Folly Frenzy could beget,
Fruits of dull Heat, and Sooterkins of Wit.
Next, o'er his Books his eyes began to roll,
In pleasing memory of all he stole,
How here he sipp'd, how there he plunder'd snug,
And suck'd all o'er, like an industrious Bug.

Here lay poor Fletcher's half-eat scenes, and here
The Frippery of crucify'd Moliere;
There hapless Shakespear, yet of Tibbald sore,
Wish'd he had blotted for himself before.
The rest on Out-side merit but presume,
Or serve (like other Fools) to fill a room;
Such with their shelves as due proportion hold,
Or their fond Parents drest in red and gold;
Or where the pictures for the page attone,
And Quarles is sav'd by Beauties not his own.
Here swells the shelf with Ogilby the great;
There, stamp'd with arms, Newcastle shines complete:
Here all his suff'ring brotherhood retire,
And 'scape the martyrdom of jakes and fire:
A Gothic Library! of Greece and Rome
Well purg'd, and worthy Settle, Banks, and Broome.
  But, high above, more solid Learning shone,
The Classics of an Age that heard of none;
There Caxton slept, with Wynkyn at his side,
One clasp'd in wood, and one in strong cow-hide;
There, sav'd by spice, like Mummies, many a year,
Dry Bodies of Divinity appear:
De Lyra there a dreadful front extends,
And here the groaning shelves Philemon bends.
  Of these twelve volumes, twelve of amplest size,
Redeem'd from tapers and defrauded pies,
Inspir'd he seizes: These an altar raise:
An hecatomb of pure, unsully'd lays
That altar crowns: A folio Common-place
Founds the whole pile, of all his works the base:
Quartos, octavos, shape the less'ning pyre;
A twisted Birth-day Ode completes the spire.
  Then he: Great Tamer of all human art!
First in my care, and ever at my heart;

Dulness! whose good old cause I yet defend,
With whom my Muse began, with whom shall end,
E'er since Sir Fopling's Periwig was Praise,
To the last honours of the Butt and Bays:
O thou! of Bus'ness the directing soul!
To this our head like byass to the bowl,
Which, as more pond'rous, made its aim more true,
Obliquely wadling to the mark in view:
O! ever gracious to perplex'd mankind,
Still spread a healing mist before the mind;
And, lest we err by Wit's wild dancing light,
Secure us kindly in our native night.
Or, if to Wit a coxcomb make pretence,
Guard the sure barrier between that and Sense;
Or quite unravel all the reas'ning thread,
And hang some curious cobweb in its stead!
As, forc'd from wind-guns, lead itself can fly,
And pond'rous slugs cut swiftly thro' the sky;
As clocks to weight their nimble motion owe,
The wheels above urg'd by the load below:
Me Emptiness, and Dulness could inspire,
And were my Elasticity, and Fire.
Some Dæmon stole my pen (forgive th' offence)
And once betray'd me into common sense:
Else all my Prose and Verse were much the same;
This, prose on stilts; that, poetry fall'n lame.
Did on the stage my Fops appear confin'd?
My Life gave ampler lessons to mankind.
Did the dead Letter unsuccessful prove?
The brisk Example never fail'd to move.
Yet sure had Heav'n decreed to save the State,
Heav'n had decreed these works a longer date.
Could Troy be sav'd by any single hand,
This grey-goose weapon must have made her stand.

What can I now? my Fletcher cast aside,
Take up the Bible, once my better guide?
Or tread the path by vent'rous Heroes trod,
This Box my Thunder, this right hand my God?
Or chair'd at White's amidst the Doctors sit,
Teach Oaths to Gamesters, and to Nobles Wit?
Or bidst thou rather Party to embrace?
(A friend to Party thou, and all her race;
'Tis the same rope at diff'rent ends they twist;
To Dulness Ridpath is as dear as Mist.)
Shall I, like Curtius, desp'rate in my zeal,
O'er head and ears plunge for the Commonweal?
Or rob Rome's ancient geese of all their glories,
And cackling save the Monarchy of Tories?
Hold—to the Minister I more incline;
To serve his cause, O Queen! is serving thine.
And see! thy very Gazetteers give o'er,
Ev'n Ralph repents, and Henly writes no more.
What then remains? Ourself. Still, still remain
Cibberian forehead, and Cibberian brain.
This brazen Brightness, to the 'Squire so dear;
This polish'd Hardness, that reflects the Peer:
This arch Absurd, that wit and fool delights;
This Mess, toss'd up of Hockley-hole and White's;
Where Dukes and Butchers join to wreathe my crown,
At once the Bear and Fiddle of the town.
  O born in sin, and forth in folly brought!
Works damn'd, or to be damn'd! (your father's fault)
Go, purify'd by flames ascend the sky,
My better and more christian progeny!
Unstain'd, untouch'd, and yet in maiden sheets;
While all your smutty sisters walk the streets.
Ye shall not beg, like gratis-given Bland,
Sent with a Pass, and vagrant thro' the land;

Not sail with Ward, to Ape-and-monkey climes,
Where vile Mundungus trucks for viler rhymes:
Not sulphur-tipt, emblaze an Ale-house fire;
Not wrap up Oranges, to pelt your sire!
O! pass more innocent, in infant state,
To the mild Limbo of our Father Tate:
Or peaceably forgot, at once be blest
In Shadwell's bosom with eternal Rest!
Soon to that mass of Nonsense to return,
Where things destroy'd are swept to things unborn.
  With that, a Tear (portentous sign of Grace!)
Stole from the Master of the sev'nfold Face:
And thrice he lifted high the Birth-day brand,
And thrice he dropt it from his quiv'ring hand;
Then lights the structure, with averted eyes:
The rowling smokes involve the sacrifice.
The op'ning clouds disclose each work by turns,
Now flames the Cid, and now Perolla burns;
Great Cæsar roars, and hisses in the fires;
King John in silence modestly expires:
No merit now the dear Nonjurer claims,
Moliere's old stubble in a moment flames.
Tears gush'd again, as from pale Priam's eyes
When the last blaze sent Ilion to the skies.
  Rowz'd by the light, old Dulness heav'd the head,
Then snatch'd a sheet of Thulè from her bed,
Sudden she flies, and whelms it o'er the pyre;
Down sink the flames, and with a hiss expire.
  Her ample presence fills up all the place;
A veil of fogs dilates her awful face:
Great in her charms! as when on Shrieves and May'rs
She looks, and breathes herself into their airs.
She bids him wait her to her sacred Dome:
Well pleas'd he enter'd, and confess'd his home.

So Spirits ending their terrestrial race,
Ascend, and recognize their Native Place.
This the Great Mother dearer held than all
The clubs of Quidnuncs, or her own Guildhall:
Here stood her Opium, here she nurs'd her Owls,
And here she plann'd th' Imperial seat of Fools.
  Here to her Chosen all her works she shews;
Prose swell'd to verse, verse loit'ring into prose:
How random thoughts now meaning chance to find,
Now leave all memory of sense behind:
How Prologues into Prefaces decay,
And these to Notes are fritter'd quite away:
How Index-learning turns no student pale,
Yet holds the eel of science by the tail:
How, with less reading than makes felons scape,
Less human genius than God gives an ape,
Small thanks to France, and none to Rome or Greece,
A past, vamp'd, future, old, reviv'd, new piece,
'Twixt Plautus, Fletcher, Shakespear, and Corneille,
Can make a Cibber, Tibbald, or Ozell.
  The Goddess then, o'er his anointed head,
With mystic words, the sacred Opium shed.
And lo! her bird, (a monster of a fowl,
Something betwixt a Heideggre and owl,)
Perch'd on his crown. 'All hail! and hail again,
My son! the promis'd land expects thy reign.
Know, Eusden thirsts no more for sack or praise;
He sleeps among the dull of ancient days;
Safe, where no Critics damn, no duns molest,
Where wretched Withers, Ward, and Gildon rest,
And high-born Howard, more majestic sire,
With Fool of Quality compleats the quire.
Thou, Cibber! thou, his Laurel shalt support,
Folly, my son, has still a Friend at Court.

Lift up your Gates, ye Princes, see him come!
Sound, sound ye Viols, be the Cat-call dumb!
Bring, bring the madding Bay, the drunken Vine;
The creeping, dirty, courtly Ivy join.
And thou! his Aid de camp, lead on my sons,
Light-arm'd with Points, Antitheses, and Puns.
Let Bawdry, Billinsgate, my daughters dear,
Support his front, and Oaths bring up the rear:
And under his, and under Archer's wing,
Gaming and Grub-street skulk behind the King.

O! when shall rise a Monarch all our own,
And I, a Nursing-mother, rock the throne;
'Twixt Prince and People close the Curtain draw,
Shade him from Light, and cover him from Law;
Fatten the Courtier, starve the learned band,
And suckle Armies, and dry-nurse the land:
'Till Senates nod to Lullabies divine,
And all be sleep, as at an Ode of thine.

She ceas'd. Then swells the Chapel-royal throat:
God save king Cibber! mounts in ev'ry note.
Familiar White's, God save king Colley! cries;
God save king Colley! Drury-lane replies:
To Needham's quick the voice triumphal rode,
But pious Needham dropt the name of God;
Back to the Devil the last echoes roll,
And Coll! each Butcher roars at Hockley-hole.
So when Jove's block descended from on high
(As sings thy great forefather Ogilby)
Loud thunder to its bottom shook the bog,
And the hoarse nation croak'd, God save King Log!

BOOK III

Lines 67–100; 317–340

Ascend this hill, whose cloudy point commands
Her boundless empire over seas and lands.
See, round the Poles where keener spangles shine,
Where spices smoke beneath the burning Line,
(Earth's wide extremes) her sable flag display'd,
And all the nations cover'd in her shade!
Far eastward cast thine eye, from whence the Sun
And orient Science their bright course begun:
One god-like Monarch all that pride confounds,
He, whose long wall the wand'ring Tartar bounds;
Heav'ns! what a pile! whole ages perish there,
And one bright blaze turns Learning into air.
Thence to the south extend thy gladden'd eyes;
There rival flames with equal glory rise,
From shelves to shelves see greedy Vulcan roll,
And lick up all their Physic of the Soul.
How little, mark! that portion of the ball,
Where, faint at best, the beams of Science fall:
Soon as they dawn, from Hyperborean skies
Embody'd dark, what clouds of Vandals rise!
Lo! where Mæotis sleeps, and hardly flows
The freezing Tanais thro' a waste of snows,
The North by myriads pours her mighty sons,
Great nurse of Goths, of Alans, and of Huns!
See Alaric's stern port! the martial frame
Of Genseric! and Attila's dread name!
See the bold Ostrogoths on Latium fall;
See the fierce Visigoths on Spain and Gaul!
See, where the morning gilds the palmy shore
(The soil that arts and infant letters bore)

His conqu'ring tribes th' Arabian prophet draws,
And saving Ignorance enthrones by Laws.
See Christians, Jews, one heavy sabbath keep,
And all the western world believe and sleep.

. . . . . .

Now Bavius take the poppy from thy brow,
And place it here! here all ye Heroes bow!
This, this is he, foretold by ancient rhymes:
Th' Augustus born to bring Saturnian times.
Signs following signs lead on the mighty year!
See! the dull stars roll round and re-appear.
See, see, our own true Phœbus wears the bays!
Our Midas sits Lord Chancellor of Plays!
On Poets Tombs see Benson's titles writ!
Lo! Ambrose Philips is prefer'd for Wit!
See under Ripley rise a new White-hall,
While Jones' and Boyle's united labours fall:
While Wren with sorrow to the grave descends,
Gay dies unpension'd with a hundred friends,
Hibernian Politics, O Swift! thy fate;
And Pope's, ten years to comment and translate.
Proceed, great days! 'till Learning fly the shore,
'Till Birch shall blush with noble blood no more,
'Till Thames see Eton's sons for ever play,
'Till Westminster's whole year be holiday,
'Till Isis' Elders reel, their pupils sport,
And Alma mater lie dissolv'd in Port?
Enough! enough! the raptur'd Monarch cries;
And thro' the Iv'ry Gate the Vision flies.

BOOK IV

The Conclusion

More she had spoke, but yawn'd—All Nature nods:
What Mortal can resist the Yawn of Gods?
Churches and Chapels instantly it reach'd;
(St. James's first, for leaden G—— preach'd)
Then catch'd the Schools; the Hall scarce kept awake;
The Convocation gap'd, but could not speak:
Lost was the Nation's Sense, nor could be found,
While the long solemn Unison went round:
Wide, and more wide, it spread o'er all the realm;
Ev'n Palinurus nodded at the Helm:
The Vapour mild o'er each Committee crept;
Unfinish'd Treaties in each Office slept;
And Chiefless Armies doz'd out the Campaign;
And Navies yawn'd for Orders on the Main.

O Muse! relate (for you can tell alone,
Wits have short Memories, and Dunces none)
Relate, who first, who last resign'd to rest;
Whose Heads she partly, whose completely blest;
What Charms could Faction, what Ambition lull,
The Venal quiet, and intrance the Dull;
'Till drown'd was Sense, and Shame, and Right, and Wrong—
O sing, and hush the Nations with thy Song!

* * * * * *

In vain, in vain,—the all-composing Hour
Resistless falls: The Muse obeys the Pow'r.
She comes! she comes! the sable Throne behold
Of *Night* Primæval, and of *Chaos* old!
Before her, *Fancy*'s gilded clouds decay,
And all its varying Rain-bows die away.

Wit shoots in vain its momentary fires,
The meteor drops, and in a flash expires.
As one by one, at dread Medea's strain,
The sick'ning stars fade off th' ethereal plain;
As Argus' eyes, by Hermes' wand opprest,
Clos'd one by one to everlasting rest;
Thus at her felt approach, and secret might,
Art after *Art* goes out, and all is Night.
See skulking *Truth* to her old cavern fled,
Mountains of Casuistry heap'd o'er her head!
Philosophy, that lean'd on Heav'n before,
Shrinks to her second cause, and is no more.
Physic of *Metaphysic* begs defence,
And *Metaphysic* calls for aid on *Sense!*
See *Mystery* to *Mathematics* fly!
In vain! they gaze, turn giddy, rave, and die.
Religion blushing veils her sacred fires,
And unawares *Morality* expires.
Nor *public* Flame, nor *private*, dares to shine;
Nor *human* Spark is left, nor Glimpse *divine!*
Lo! thy dread Empire, CHAOS! is restor'd;
Light dies before thy uncreating word:
Thy hand, great Anarch! lets the curtain fall;
And universal Darkness buries All.

Of the

Use of Riches,

An Epistle to the Right Honourable

Allen Lord Bathurst

1732

The Duke of Buckingham

Lines 299–314

In the worst inn's worst room, with mat half-hung,
The floors of plaister, and the walls of dung,
On once a flock-bed, but repair'd with straw,
With tape-ty'd curtains, never meant to draw,
The George and Garter dangling from that bed
Where tawdry yellow strove with dirty red,
Great Villiers lies—alas! how chang'd from him,
That life of pleasure, and that soul of whim!
Gallant and gay, in Cliveden's proud alcove,
The bow'r of wanton Shrewsbury and love;
Or just as gay, at Council, in a ring
Of mimick'd Statesmen, and their merry King.
No Wit to flatter, left of all his store!
No Fool to laugh at, which he valu'd more.
There, Victor of his health, of fortune, friends,
And fame; this lord of useless thousands ends.

The First Satire of the Second Book of Horace

Imitated in a Dialogue between Alexander Pope of Twickenham on the one Part, and his Learned Council [William Fortescue] on the other

1733

P. THERE are (I scarce can think it, but am told)
There are, to whom my Satire seems too bold:
Scarce to wise Peter complaisant enough,
And something said of Chartres much too rough.
The lines are weak, another's pleas'd to say,
Lord Fanny spins a thousand such a day.
Tim'rous by nature, of the Rich in awe,
I come to Council learned in the Law:
You'll give me, like a friend both sage and free,
Advice; and (as you use) without a Fee.
F. I'd write no more.
P. Not write? but then I think,
And for my soul I cannot sleep a wink.
I nod in company, I wake at night,
Fools rush into my head, and so I write.
F. You could not do a worse thing for your life.
Why, if the nights seem tedious—take a Wife:
Or rather truly, if your point be rest,
Lettuce and cowslip-wine; *Probatum est*.
But talk with Celsus, Celsus will advise
Hartshorn, or something that shall close your eyes.
Or, if you needs must write, write CAESAR'S Praise,
You'll gain at least a *Knighthood*, or the *Bays*.
P. What? like Sir Richard, rumbling, rough, and fierce,
With ARMS, and GEORGE, and BRUNSWICK crowd the verse,

Rend with tremendous sound your ears asunder,
With Gun, Drum, Trumpet, Blunderbuss, and Thunder?
Or nobly wild, with Budgel's fire and force,
Paint Angels trembling round his falling Horse?
F. Then all your Muse's softer art display,
Let CAROLINA smooth the tuneful lay,
Lull with AMELIA's liquid name the Nine,
And sweetly flow thro' all the Royal Line.
P. Alas! few verses touch their nicer ear;
They scarce can bear their *Laureate* twice a year;
And justly CAESAR scorns the Poet's lays,
It is to *History* he trusts for Praise.
F. Better be Cibber, I'll maintain it still,
Than ridicule all Taste, blaspheme Quadrille,
Abuse the City's best good men in metre,
And laugh at Peers that put their trust in Peter.
Ev'n those you touch not, hate you.
P. What should ail them?
F. A hundred smart in Timon and in Balaam:
The fewer still you name, you wound the more;
Bond is but one, but Harpax is a score.
P. Each mortal has his pleasure: none deny
Scarsdale his bottle, Darty his Ham-pye;
Ridotta sips and dances, till she see
The doubling Lustres dance as fast as she;
F— loves the Senate, Hockley-hole his brother,
Like in all else, as one Egg to another.
I love to pour out all my self, as plain
As downright SHIPPEN, or as old Montagne:
In them, as certain to be lov'd as seen,
The Soul stood forth, nor kept a thought within;
In me what spots (for spots I have) appear,
Will prove at least the Medium must be clear.
In this impartial glass, my Muse intends

Fair to expose myself, my foes, my friends;
Publish the present age; but where my text
Is Vice too high, reserve it for the next:
My foes shall wish my life a longer date,
And ev'ry friend the less lament my fate.
My head and heart thus flowing thro' my quill,
Verse-man or Prose-man, term me which you will,
Papist or Protestant, or both between,
Like good Erasmus in an honest Mean,
In moderation placing all my glory,
While Tories call me Whig, and Whigs a Tory.
  Satire's my weapon, but I'm too discreet
To run amuck, and tilt at all I meet;
I only wear it in a land of Hectors,
Thieves, Supercargoes, Sharpers, and Directors.
Save but our *Army!* and let Jove incrust
Swords, pikes, and guns, with everlasting rust!
Peace is my dear delight—not FLEURY'S more:
But touch me, and no Minister so sore.
Whoe'er offends, at some unlucky time
Slides into verse, and hitches in a rhyme,
Sacred to Ridicule his whole life long,
And the sad burthen of some merry song.
  Slander or Poison dread from Delia's rage,
Hard words or hanging, if your Judge be Page.
From furious Sappho scarce a milder fate,
P-x'd by her love, or libell'd by her hate.
Its proper pow'r to hurt, each creature feels;
Bulls aim their horns, and Asses lift their heels;
'Tis a Bear's talent not to kick, but hug;
And no man wonders he's not stung by Pug.
So drink with Walters, or with Chartres eat,
They'll never poison you, they'll only cheat.
Then, learned Sir! (to cut the matter short)

Whate'er my fate, or well or ill at Court,
Whether Old age, with faint but chearful ray,
Attends to gild the Ev'ning of my day,
Or Death's black wing already be display'd,
To wrap me in the universal shade;
Whether the darken'd room to muse invite,
Or whiten'd wall provoke the skew'r to write:
In durance, exile, Bedlam, or the Mint,
Like Lee or Budgell, I will rhyme and print.
F. Alas young man! your days can ne'er be long,
In flow'r of age you perish for a song!
Plums and Directors, Shylock and his Wife,
Will club their Testers, now, to take your life!
P. What? arm'd for Virtue when I point the pen,
Brand the bold front of shameless guilty men;
Dash the proud Gamester in his gilded Car;
Bare the mean Heart that lurks beneath a *Star*;
Can there be wanting, to defend Her cause,
Lights of the Church, or Guardians of the Laws?
Could pension'd Boileau lash in honest strain
Flatt'rers and Bigots ev'n in Louis' reign?
Could Laureate Dryden Pimp and Fry'r engage,
Yet neither Charles nor James be in a rage?
And I not strip the gilding off a Knave,
Unplac'd, unpension'd, no man's heir, or slave?
I will, or perish in the gen'rous cause:
Hear this, and tremble! you, who 'scape the Laws.
Yes, while I live, no rich or noble knave
Shall walk the World, in credit, to his grave.
To VIRTUE ONLY and HER FRIENDS A FRIEND,
The World beside may murmur, or commend.
Know, all the distant din that world can keep,
Rolls o'er my Grotto, and but sooths my sleep.
There, my retreat the best Companions grace,

Chiefs out of war, and Statesmen out of place.
There St. John mingles with my friendly bowl
The Feast of Reason and the Flow of soul:
And He, whose lightning pierc'd th' Iberian Lines,
Now forms my Quincunx, and now ranks my Vines,
Or tames the Genius of the stubborn plain,
Almost as quickly as he conquer'd Spain.
Envy must own, I live among the Great,
No Pimp of pleasure, and no Spy of state,
With eyes that pry not, tongue that ne'er repeats,
Fond to spread friendships, but to cover heats;
To help who want, to forward who excel;
This, all who know me, know; who love me, tell;
And who unknown defame me, let them be
Scriblers or Peers, alike are *Mob* to me.
This is my plea, on this I rest my cause—
What saith my Council, learned in the laws?
F. Your Plea is good; but still I say, beware!
Laws are explain'd by Men—so have a care.
It stands on record, that in Richard's times
A man was hang'd for very honest rhymes.
Consult the Statute: *quart.* I think, it is,
Edwardi sext. or *prim. et quint. Eliz.*
See *Libels, Satires*—here you have it—read.
P. Libels and *Satires!* lawless things indeed!
But grave *Epistles*, bringing Vice to light,
Such as a King might read, a Bishop write,
Such as Sir Robert would approve—
F. Indeed?
The Case is alter'd—you may then proceed;
In such a cause the Plaintiff will be hiss'd,
My Lords the Judges laugh, and you're dismiss'd.

AN ESSAY ON MAN
in the Epistles to a Friend

1733, 4

EPISTLE I
The Beginning

Lines 1–112

AWAKE, my ST. JOHN! leave all meaner things
To low ambition, and the pride of Kings.
Let us (since Life can little more supply
Than just to look about us and to die)
Expatiate free o'er all this scene of Man;
A mighty maze! but not without a plan;
A Wild, where weeds and flow'rs promiscuous shoot;
Or Garden, tempting with forbidden fruit.
Together let us beat this ample field,
Try what the open, what the covert yield;
The latent tracts, the giddy heights, explore
Of all who blindly creep, or sightless soar;
Eye Nature's walks, shoot Folly as it flies,
And catch the Manners living as they rise;
Laugh where we must, be candid where we can;
But vindicate the ways of God to Man.
 Say first, of God above, or Man below,
What can we reason, but from what we know?
Of Man, what see we but his station here,
From which to reason, or to which refer?
Thro' worlds unnumber'd tho' the God be known,
'Tis ours to trace him only in our own.
He, who thro' vast immensity can pierce,
See worlds on worlds compose one universe,
Observe how system into system runs,
What other planets circle other suns,

What vary'd Being peoples ev'ry star,
May tell why Heav'n has made us as we are.
But of this frame the bearings, and the ties,
The strong connections, nice dependencies,
Gradations just, has thy pervading soul
Look'd thro'? or can a part contain the whole?
  Is the great chain, that draws all to agree,
And drawn supports, upheld by God, or thee?
  Presumptuous Man! the reason wouldst thou find,
Why form'd so weak, so little, and so blind?
First, if thou canst, the harder reason guess,
Why form'd no weaker, blinder, and no less?
Ask of thy mother earth, why oaks are made
Taller or stronger than the weeds they shade?
Or ask of yonder argent fields above,
Why JOVE's Satellites are less than JOVE?
  Of Systems possible, if 'tis confest
That Wisdom infinite must form the best,
Where all must full or not coherent be,
And all that rises, rise in due degree;
Then, in the scale of reas'ning life, 'tis plain,
There must be, somewhere, such a rank as Man:
And all the question (wrangle e'er so long)
Is only this, if God has plac'd him wrong?
  Respecting Man, whatever wrong we call,
May, must be right, as relative to all.
In human works, tho' labour'd on with pain,
A thousand movements scarce one purpose gain;
In God's, one single can its end produce;
Yet serves to second too some other use.
So Man, who here seems principal alone,
Perhaps acts second to some sphere unknown,
Touches some wheel, or verges to some goal;
'Tis but a part we see, and not a whole.

III

When the proud steed shall know why Man restrains
His fiery course, or drives him o'er the plains;
When the dull Ox, why now he breaks the clod,
Is now a victim, and now Ægypt's God:
Then shall Man's pride and dulness comprehend
His actions', passions', being's, use and end;
Why doing, suff'ring, check'd, impell'd; and why
This hour a slave, the next a deity.

Then say not Man's imperfect, Heav'n in fault;
Say rather, Man's as perfect as he ought:
His knowledge measur'd to his state and place;
His time a moment, and a point his space.
If to be perfect in a certain sphere,
What matter, soon or late, or here or there?
The blest to day is as completely so,
As who began a thousand years ago.

Heav'n from all creatures hides the book of Fate,
All but the page prescrib'd, their present state:
From brutes what men, from men what spirits know:
Or who could suffer Being here below?
The lamb thy riot dooms to bleed to-day,
Had he thy Reason, would he skip and play?
Pleas'd to the last, he crops the flow'ry food,
And licks the hand just rais'd to shed his blood.
Oh blindness to the future! kindly giv'n,
That each may fill the circle mark'd by Heav'n:
Who sees with equal eye, as God of all,
A hero perish, or a sparrow fall,
Atoms or systems into ruin hurl'd,
And now a bubble burst, and now a world.

Hope humbly then; with trembling pinions soar;
Wait the great teacher Death; and God adore.
What future bliss, he gives not thee to know,
But gives that Hope to be thy blessing now.

Hope springs eternal in the human breast:
Man never Is, but always To be blest:
The soul, uneasy and confin'd from home,
Rests and expatiates in a life to come.
Lo, the poor Indian! whose untutor'd mind
Sees God in clouds, or hears him in the wind;
His soul, proud Science never taught to stray
Far as the solar walk, or milky way;
Yet simple Nature to his hope has giv'n,
Behind the cloud-topt hill, an humbler heav'n;
Some safer world in depth of woods embrac'd,
Some happier island in the wat'ry waste,
Where slaves once more their native land behold,
No fiends torment, no Christians thirst for gold.
To Be, contents his natural desire,
He asks no Angel's wing, no Seraph's fire;
But thinks, admitted to that equal sky,
His faithful dog shall bear him company.

EPISTLE IV

The Conclusion

Lines 373–398

Come then, my Friend! my Genius! come along;
Oh master of the poet, and the song!
And while the Muse now stoops, or now ascends,
To Man's low passions, or their glorious ends,
Teach me, like thee, in various nature wise,
To fall with dignity, with temper rise;
Form'd by thy converse, happily to steer
From grave to gay, from lively to severe;
Correct with spirit, eloquent with ease,
Intent to reason, or polite to please.

Oh! while along the stream of Time thy name
Expanded flies, and gathers all its fame,
Say, shall my little bark attendant sail,
Pursue the triumph, and partake the gale?
When statesmen, heroes, kings, in dust repose,
Whose sons shall blush their fathers were thy foes,
Shall then this verse to future age pretend
Thou wert my guide, philosopher, and friend?
That urg'd by thee, I turn'd the tuneful art
From sounds to things, from fancy to the heart;
For Wit's false mirror held up Nature's light;
Shew'd erring Pride, WHATEVER IS, IS RIGHT;
That REASON, PASSION, answer one great aim;
That true SELF-LOVE and SOCIAL are the same;
That VIRTUE only makes our Bliss below;
And all our Knowledge is, OURSELVES TO KNOW.

A N

E P I S T L E

F R O M

Mr. *P O P E*,

T O

Dr. *A R B U T H N O T*.

Neque ſermonibus Vulgi *dederis te, nec in* Præmiis *humanis ſpem poſueris rerum tuarum: ſuis te oportet illecebris* ipſa Virtus *trahat ad verum decus. Quid de te alii loquantur, ipſi videant, ſed loquentur tamen.*

TULLY.

L O N D O N:

Printed by *J. Wright* for LAWTON GILLIVER at *Homer*'s *Head* in *Fleetſtreet*, 1734.

An Epistle to DR. ARBUTHNOT

ADVERTISEMENT to

The first publication of this Epistle

THIS paper is a sort of bill of complaint, begun many years since, and drawn up by snatches, as the several occasions offered. I had no thoughts of publishing it, till it pleased some Persons of Rank and Fortune [the Authors of *Verses to the Imitator of Horace*, and of an *Epistle to a Doctor of Divinity from a Nobleman at Hampton Court*] to attack, in a very extraordinary manner, not only my Writings (of which, being public, the Public is judge) but my *Person, Morals*, and *Family*, whereof, to those who know me not, a truer information may be requisite. Being divided between the necessity to say something of *myself*, and my own laziness to undertake so awkward a task, I thought it the shortest way to put the last hand to this Epistle. If it have any thing pleasing, it will be that by which I am most desirous to please, the *Truth* and the *Sentiment*; and if any thing offensive, it will be only to those I am least sorry to offend, *the vicious* or *the ungenerous*.

Many will know their own pictures in it, there being not a circumstance but what is true; but I have, for the most part, spared their *Names*, and they may escape being laughed at, if they please.

I would have some of them know, it was owing to the request of the learned and candid Friend to whom it is inscribed, that I make not as free use of theirs as they have done of mine. However, I shall have this advantage, and honour, on my side, that whereas, by their proceeding, any abuse may be directed at any man, no injury can possibly be done by mine, since a nameless Character can never be found out, but by its *truth* and *likeness*. P.

P. Shut, shut the door, good John! fatigu'd I said,
Tye up the knocker, say I'm sick, I'm dead.
The Dog-star rages! nay 'tis past a doubt,
All Bedlam, or Parnassus, is let out:
Fire in each eye, and papers in each hand,
They rave, recite, and madden round the land.
What walls can guard me, or what shades can hide?
They pierce my thickets, thro' my Grot they glide,
By land, by water, they renew the charge,
They stop the chariot, and they board the barge.
No place is sacred, not the Church is free,
Ev'n Sunday shines no Sabbath-day to me:
Then from the Mint walks forth the Man of rhyme,
Happy! to catch me, just at Dinner-time.
Is there a Parson, much be-mus'd in beer,
A maudlin Poetess, a rhyming Peer,
A Clerk, foredoom'd his father's soul to cross,
Who pens a Stanza, when he should *engross?*
Is there, who, lock'd from ink and paper, scrawls
With desp'rate charcoal round his darken'd walls?
All fly to Twit'nam, and in humble strain
Apply to me, to keep them mad or vain.
Arthur, whose giddy son neglects the Laws,
Imputes to me and my damn'd works the cause:
Poor Cornus sees his frantic wife elope,
And curses Wit, and Poetry, and Pope.
Friend to my Life! (which did not you prolong,
The world had wanted many an idle song)
What *Drop* or *Nostrum* can this plague remove?
Or which must end me, a Fool's wrath or love?

A dire dilemma! either way I'm sped,
If foes, they write, if friends, they read me dead.
Seiz'd and ty'd down to judge, how wretched I!
Who can't be silent, and who will not lye:
To laugh, were want of goodness and of grace,
And to be grave, exceeds all Pow'r of face.
I sit with sad civility, I read
With honest anguish, and an aching head;
And drop at last, but in unwilling ears,
This saving counsel, 'Keep your piece nine years.'
  Nine years! cries he, who high in Drury-lane,
Lull'd by soft Zephyrs thro' the broken pane,
Rhymes ere he wakes, and prints before *Term* ends,
Oblig'd by hunger, and request of friends:
'The piece, you think, is incorrect? why take it,
'I'm all submission, what you'd have it, make it.'
  Three things another's modest wishes bound,
My Friendship, and a Prologue, and ten Pound.
  Pitholeon sends to me: 'You know his Grace,
'I want a Patron; ask him for a Place.'
Pitholeon libell'd me—'but here 's a letter
'Informs you, Sir, 'twas when he knew no better.
'Dare you refuse him? Curl invites to dine,
'He'll write a *Journal*, or he'll turn Divine.'
  Bless me! a packet.—''Tis a stranger sues,
'A Virgin Tragedy, an Orphan Muse.'
If I dislike it, 'Furies, death and rage!'
If I approve, 'Commend it to the Stage.'
There (thank my stars) my whole commission ends,
The Play'rs and I are, luckily, no friends.
Fir'd that the house reject him, ''Sdeath I'll print it,
'And shame the fools—Your int'rest, Sir, with Lintot.'
Lintot, dull rogue! will think your price too much:
'Not, Sir, if you revise it, and retouch.'

All my demurs but double his attacks;
At last he whispers, 'Do; and we go snacks.'
Glad of a quarrel, strait I clap the door,
Sir, let me see your works and you no more.
'Tis sung, when Midas' Ears began to spring,
(Midas, a sacred person and a King)
His very Minister who spy'd them first,
(Some say his Queen) was forc'd to speak, or burst.
And is not mine, my friend, a sorer case,
When ev'ry coxcomb perks them in my face?
A. Good friend forbear! you deal in dang'rous things.
I'd never name Queens, Ministers, or Kings;
Keep close to Ears, and those let asses prick,
'Tis nothing—*P*. Nothing? if they bite and kick?
Out with it, DUNCIAD! let the secret pass,
That secret to each fool, that he's an Ass:
The truth once told (and wherefore should we lie?)
The Queen of Midas slept, and so may I.
You think this cruel? take it for a rule,
No creature smarts so little as a fool.
Let peals of laughter, Codrus! round thee break,
Thou unconcern'd canst hear the mighty crack:
Pit, box, and gall'ry in convulsions hurl'd,
Thou stand'st unshook amidst a bursting world.
Who shames a Scribler? break one cobweb thro',
He spins the slight, self-pleasing thread anew:
Destroy his fib or sophistry, in vain,
The creature's at his dirty work again,
Thron'd in the centre of his thin designs,
Proud of a vast extent of flimzy lines!
Whom have I hurt? has Poet yet, or Peer,
Lost the arch'd eye-brow, or Parnassian sneer?
And has not Colly still his lord, and whore?
His butchers Henley, his free-masons Moor?

Does not one table Bavius still admit
Still to one Bishop Philips seem a wit?
Still Sappho—*A*. Hold! for God-sake—you'll offend,
No Names—be calm—learn prudence of a friend:
I too could write, and I am twice as tall;
But foes like these—*P*. One Flatt'rer's worse than all.
Of all mad creatures, if the learn'd are right,
It is the slaver kills, and not the bite.
A fool quite angry is quite innocent:
Alas! 'tis ten times worse when they *repent.*
  One dedicates in high heroic prose,
And ridicules beyond a hundred foes:
One from all Grubstreet will my fame defend,
And more abusive, calls himself my friend.
This prints my *Letters*, that expects a bribe,
And others roar aloud, 'Subscribe, subscribe.'
  There are, who to my person pay their court:
I cough like *Horace*, and, tho' lean, am short,
Ammon's great son one shoulder had too high,
Such *Ovid's* nose, and 'Sir! you have an Eye'—
Go on, obliging creatures, make me see
All that disgrac'd my Betters, met in me.
Say for my comfort, languishing in bed,
'Just so immortal *Maro* held his head:'
And when I die, be sure you let me know
Great *Homer* dy'd three thousand years ago.
  Why did I write? what sin to me unknown
Dipt me in ink, my parents', or my own?
As yet a child, nor yet a fool to fame,
I lisp'd in numbers, for the numbers came.
I left no calling for this idle trade,
No duty broke, no father disobey'd.
The Muse but serv'd to ease some friend, not Wife,
To help me thro' this long disease, my Life,

To second, ARBUTHNOT! thy Art and Care,
And teach, the Being you preserv'd, to bear.
  But why then publish? *Granville* the polite,
And knowing *Walsh,* would tell me I could write;
Well-natur'd *Garth* inflam'd with early praise,
And *Congreve* lov'd, and *Swift* endur'd my lays;
The courtly *Talbot, Somers, Sheffield* read,
Ev'n mitred *Rochester* would nod the head,
And *St. John's* self (great *Dryden's* friends before)
With open arms receiv'd one Poet more.
Happy my studies, when by these approv'd!
Happier their author, when by these belov'd!
From these the world will judge of men and books,
Not from the *Burnets, Oldmixons,* and *Cooks.*
  Soft were my numbers; who could take offence
While pure Description held the place of Sense?
Like gentle *Fanny's* was my flow'ry theme,
A painted mistress, or a purling stream.
Yet then did *Gildon* draw his venal quill;
I wish'd the man a dinner, and sate still.
Yet then did *Dennis* rave in furious fret;
I never answer'd, I was not in debt.
If want provok'd, or madness made them print,
I wag'd no war with *Bedlam* or the *Mint.*
  Did some more sober Critic come abroad;
If wrong, I smil'd; if right, I kiss'd the rod.
Pains, reading, study, are their just pretence,
And all they want is spirit, taste, and sense.
Comma's and points they set exactly right,
And 'twere a sin to rob them of their mite.
Yet ne'er one sprig of laurel grac'd these ribalds,
From slashing *Bentley* down to pidling *Tibalds:*
Each wight, who reads not, and but scans and spells,
Each Word-catcher, that lives on syllables,

Ev'n such small Critics some regard may claim,
Preserv'd in *Milton's* or in *Shakespear's* name.
Pretty! in amber to observe the forms
Of hairs, or straws, or dirt, or grubs, or worms!
The things, we know, are neither rich nor rare,
But wonder how the devil they got there.
  Were others angry? I excus'd them too;
Well might they rage, I gave them but their due.
A man's true merit 'tis not hard to find;
But each man's secret standard in his mind,
That casting-weight Pride adds to Emptiness,
This, who can gratify? for who can *guess?*
The Bard whom pilfer'd Pastorals renown,
Who turns a Persian tale for half a crown,
Just writes to make his barrenness appear,
And strains from hard-bound brains, eight lines a year;
He, who still wanting, tho' he lives on theft,
Steals much, spends little, yet has nothing left:
And He, who now to sense, now nonsense leaning,
Means not, but blunders round about a meaning:
And He, whose fustian 's so sublimely bad,
It is not Poetry, but prose run mad:
All these, my modest Satire bad *translate*,
And own'd that nine such Poets made a *Tate*.
How did they fume, and stamp, and roar, and chafe!
And swear, not ADDISON himself was safe.
  Peace to all such! but were there One whose fires
True Genius kindles, and fair Fame inspires;
Blest with each talent and each art to please,
And born to write, converse, and live with ease:
Should such a man, too fond to rule alone,
Bear, like the Turk, no brother near the throne,
View him with scornful, yet with jealous eyes,
And hate for arts that caus'd himself to rise;

Damn with faint praise, assent with civil leer,
And without sneering, teach the rest to sneer;
Willing to wound, and yet afraid to strike,
Just hint a fault, and hesitate dislike;
Alike reserv'd to blame, or to commend,
A tim'rous foe, and a suspicious friend;
Dreading ev'n fools, by Flatterers besieg'd,
And so obliging, that he ne'er oblig'd;
Like *Cato*, give his little Senate laws,
And sit attentive to his own applause;
While Wits and Templars ev'ry sentence raise,
And wonder with a foolish face of praise—
Who but must laugh, if such a man there be?
Who would not weep, if ATTICUS were he!
What tho' my Name stood rubric on the walls,
Or plaister'd posts, with claps, in capitals?
Or smoaking forth, a hundred hawkers load,
On wings of winds came flying all abroad?
I sought no homage from the Race that write;
I kept, like *Asian* Monarchs, from their sight:
Poems I heeded (now be-rhym'd so long) .
No more than thou, great GEORGE! a birth-day song.
I ne'er with wits or witlings pass'd my days,
To spread about the itch of verse and praise;
Nor like a puppy, daggled thro' the town,
To fetch and carry sing-song up and down;
Nor at Rehearsals sweat, and mouth'd, and cry'd,
With handkerchief and orange at my side;
But sick of fops, and poetry, and prate,
To *Bufo* left the whole *Castalian* state.
Proud as *Apollo* on his forked hill,
Sate full-blown *Bufo*, puff'd by ev'ry quill;
Fed with soft Dedication all day long,
Horace and he went hand in hand in song.

His Library (where busts of Poets dead
And a true *Pindar* stood without a head)
Receiv'd of wits an undistinguish'd race,
Who first his judgment ask'd, and then a place:
Much they extoll'd his pictures, much his seat,
And flatter'd ev'ry day, and some days eat:
Till grown more frugal in his riper days,
He paid some bards with port, and some with praise,
To some a dry rehearsal was assign'd,
And others (harder still) he paid in kind.
Dryden alone (what wonder?) came not nigh,
Dryden alone escap'd this judging eye:
But still the *Great* have kindness in reserve,
He help'd to bury whom he help'd to starve.
  May some choice Patron bless each gray goose quill!
May ev'ry *Bavius* have his *Bufo* still!
So when a Statesman wants a day's defence,
Or Envy holds a whole week's war with Sense,
Or simple Pride for Flatt'ry makes demands,
May dunce by dunce be whistled off my hands!
Blest be the *Great!* for those they take away,
And those they left me; for they left me GAY;
Left me to see neglected Genius bloom,
Neglected die, and tell it on his tomb:
Of all thy blameless life the sole return
My Verse, and QUEENSB'RY weeping o'er thy urn!
  Oh let me live my own, and die so too!
(To live and die is all I have to do:)
Maintain a Poet's dignity and ease,
And see what friends, and read what books I please:
Above a Patron, tho' I condescend
Sometimes to call a Minister my friend.
I was not born for Courts or great affairs;
I pay my debts, believe, and say my pray'rs;

Can sleep without a Poem in my head,
Nor know, if *Dennis* be alive or dead.
  Why am I ask'd what next shall see the light?
Heav'ns! was I born for nothing but to write?
Has Life no joys for me? or (to be grave)
Have I no friend to serve, no soul to save?
'I found him close with *Swift'*—'Indeed? no doubt'
(Cries prating *Balbus*) 'something will come out.'
'Tis all in vain, deny it as I will.
'No, such a Genius never can lie still';
And then for mine obligingly mistakes
The first Lampoon Sir *Will.* or *Bubo* makes.
Poor guiltless I! and can I chuse but smile,
When ev'ry Coxcomb knows me by my *Style?*
  Curst be the verse, how well soe'er it flow,
That tends to make one worthy man my foe,
Give Virtue scandal, Innocence a fear,
Or from the soft-ey'd Virgin steal a tear!
But he who hurts a harmless neighbour's peace,
Insults fall'n worth, or Beauty in distress,
Who loves a Lye, lame slander helps about,
Who writes a Libel, or who copies out:
That Fop, whose pride affects a patron's name,
Yet absent, wounds an author's honest fame:
Who can *your* merit *selfishly* approve,
And show the *sense* of it without the *love*;
Who has the vanity to call you friend,
Yet wants the honour, injur'd, to defend;
Who tells whate'er you think, whate'er you say,
And, if he lye not, must at least betray:
Who to the *Dean*, and *silver bell* can swear,
And sees at *Cannons* what was never there;
Who reads, but with a lust to misapply,
Make Satire a Lampoon, and Fiction Lye.

A lash like mine no honest man shall dread,
But all such babbling blockheads in his stead.
  Let *Sporus* tremble—*A*. What? that thing of silk,
Sporus, that mere white curd of Ass's milk?
Satire or sense, alas! can *Sporus* feel?
Who breaks a butterfly upon a wheel?
P. Yet let me flap this bug with gilded wings,
This painted child of dirt, that stinks and stings;
Whose buzz the witty and the fair annoys,
Yet wit ne'er tastes, and beauty ne'er enjoys:
So well-bred spaniels civilly delight
In mumbling of the game they dare not bite.
Eternal smiles his emptiness betray,
As shallow streams run dimpling all the way.
Whether in florid impotence he speaks,
And, as the prompter breathes, the puppet squeaks;
Or at the ear of *Eve*, familiar Toad,
Half froth, half venom, spits himself abroad,
In puns, or politics, or tales, or lies,
Or spite, or smut, or rhymes, or blasphemies.
His wit all see-saw, between *that* and *this*,
Now high, now low, now master up, now miss,
And he himself one vile Antithesis.
Amphibious thing! that acting either part,
The trifling head, or the corrupted heart,
Fop at the toilet, flatt'rer at the board,
Now trips a Lady, and now struts a Lord.
Eve's tempter thus the Rabbins have exprest,
A Cherub's face, a reptile all the rest,
Beauty that shocks you, parts that none will trust,
Wit that can creep, and pride that licks the dust.
  Not Fortune's worshipper, nor Fashion's fool,
Not Lucre's madman, nor Ambition's tool,
Not proud, nor servile; Be one Poet's praise,

That, if he pleas'd, he pleas'd by manly ways:
That Flatt'ry, ev'n to King's, he held a shame,
And thought a Lye in verse or prose the same.
That not in Fancy's maze he wander'd long,
But stoop'd to Truth, and moraliz'd his song:
That not for Fame, but Virtue's better end,
He stood the furious foe, the timid friend,
The damning critic, half approving wit,
The coxcomb hit, or fearing to be hit;
Laugh'd at the loss of friends he never had,
The dull, the proud, the wicked, and the mad;
The distant threats of vengeance on his head,
The blow unfelt, the tear he never shed;
The tale reviv'd, the lye so oft o'erthrown,
Th' imputed trash, and dulness not his own;
The morals blacken'd when the writings scape,
The libel'd person, and the pictur'd shape;
Abuse, on all he lov'd, or lov'd him, spread,
A friend in exile, or a father, dead;
The whisper, that to greatness still too near,
Perhaps, yet vibrates on his SOV'REIGN'S ear—
Welcome for thee, fair Virtue! all the past:
For thee, fair Virtue! welcome ev'n the *last!*
A. But why insult the poor, affront the great?
P. A knave 's a knave, to me, in ev'ry state:
Alike my scorn, if he succeed or fail,
Sporus at court, or *Japhet* in a jail,
A hireling scribbler, or a hireling peer,
Knight of the post corrupt, or of the shire;
If on a Pillory, or near a Throne,
He gain his Prince's ear, or lose his own.
Yet soft by nature, more a dupe than wit,
Sappho can tell you how this man was bit:
This dreaded Sat'rist *Dennis* will confess

Foe to his pride, but friend to his distress:
So humble, he has knock'd at *Tibbald's* door,
Has drunk with *Cibber*, nay has rhym'd for *Moor.*
Full ten years slander'd, did he once reply?
Three thousand suns went down on *Welsted's* lye.
To please a Mistress one aspers'd his life;
He lash'd him not, but let her be his wife:
Let *Budgel* charge low *Grubstreet* on his quill,
And write whate'er he pleas'd, except his Will;
Let the two *Curls* of Town and Court, abuse
His father, mother, body, soul, and muse.
Yet why? that Father held it for a rule,
It was a sin to call our neighbour fool:
That harmless Mother thought no wife a whore:
Hear this, and spare his family, *James Moore!*
Unspotted names, and memorable long!
If there be force in Virtue, or in Song.
  Of gentle blood (part shed in Honour's cause,
While yet in *Britain* Honour had applause)
Each parent sprung—*A*. What fortune, pray?—
      P. Their own,
And better got, than *Bestia's* from the throne.
Born to no Pride, inheriting no Strife,
Nor marrying Discord in a noble wife,
Stranger to civil and religious rage,
The good man walk'd innoxious thro' his age.
No Courts he saw, no suits would ever try,
Nor dar'd an Oath, nor hazarded a Lye.
Un-learn'd, he knew no schoolman's subtile art,
No language, but the language of the heart.
By Nature honest, by Experience wise,
Healthy by temp'rance, and by exercise;
His life, tho' long, to sickness past unknown.
His death was instant, and without a groan.

O grant me, thus to live, and thus to die!
Who sprung from Kings shall know less joy than I.
  O Friend! may each domestic bliss be thine!
Be no unpleasing Melancholy mine:
Me, let the tender office long engage,
To rock the cradle of reposing Age,
With lenient arts extend a Mother's breath,
Make Langour smile, and smooth the bed of Death,
Explore the thought, explain the asking eye,
And keep a while one parent from the sky!
On cares like these if length of days attend,
May Heav'n, to bless those days, preserve my Friend,
Preserve him social, chearful, and serene,
And just as rich as when he serv'd a QUEEN.
A. Whether that blessing be deny'd or giv'n,
Thus far was right, the rest belongs to Heav'n.

The First Epistle of the Second Book of Horace, Imitated

1737

ADVERTISEMENT

THE Reflections of *Horace*, and the Judgments past in his Epistle to *Augustus*, seem'd so seasonable to the present Times, that I could not help applying them to the use of my own Country. The Author thought them considerable enough to address them to his Prince; whom he paints with all the great and good qualities of a Monarch, upon whom the Romans depended for the Encrease of an *Absolute Empire*. But to make the Poem entirely English, I was willing to add one or two of those which contribute to the Happiness of a *Free People*, and are more consistent with the Welfare of *our Neighbours*.

This Epistle will show the learned World to have fallen into two mistakes: one, that *Augustus was a Patron of Poets in general*; whereas he not only prohibited all but the Best Writers to name him, but recommended that Care even to the Civil Magistrate: *Admonebat Praetores, ne paterentur Nomen suum obsolefieri*, etc. The other, that this Piece was only a *general Discourse of Poetry*; whereas it was an *Apology for the Poets*, in order to render *Augustus* more their Patron. *Horace* here pleads the Cause of his Cotemporaries, first against the Taste of the *Town*, whose humour it was to magnify the Authors of the preceding Age; secondly against the *Court* and *Nobility*, who encouraged only the Writers for the Theatre; and lastly against the *Emperor* himself, who had conceived them of little Use to the Government. He shews (by a View of the Progress of Learning, and the Change of Taste among the Romans) that the Introduction of the Polite Arts of *Greece* had given the Writers of his Time great advantages over their Predecessors; that their *Morals* were much improved, and the Licence of those ancient Poets restrained; that *Satire* and *Comedy* were become more just and useful; that whatever extravagancies were left on the Stage, were owing to the *Ill Taste* of the *Nobility*; that Poets, under due Regulations, were in many respects useful to the *State*, and concludes, that it was upon them the *Emperor* himself must depend, for his Fame with Posterity.

We may farther learn from this Epistle, that *Horace* made his Court to this Great Prince by writing with a decent Freedom towards him, with a just Contempt of his low Flatterers, and with a manly Regard to his own Character.

EPISTLE I

To AUGUSTUS

WHILE you, great Patron of Mankind, sustain
The balanc'd World, and open all the Main;
Your Country, chief, in Arms abroad defend,
At home, with Morals, Arts, and Laws amend;
How shall the Muse, from such a Monarch, steal
An hour, and not defraud the Public Weal?
  Edward and Henry, now the Boast of Fame,
And virtuous Alfred, a more sacred Name,
After a Life of gen'rous Toils endur'd,
The Gaul subdu'd, or Property secur'd,
Ambition humbled, mighty Cities storm'd,
Or Laws establish'd, and the World reform'd;
Clos'd their long Glories with a sigh, to find
Th' unwilling Gratitude of base mankind!

All human Virtue, to its latest breath,
Finds Envy never conquer'd, but by Death.
The great Alcides, ev'ry Labour past,
Had still this Monster to subdue at last.
Sure fate of all, beneath whose rising ray
Each star of meaner merit fades away;
Oppress'd we feel the beam directly beat,
Those Suns of Glory please not till they set.
  To Thee, the World its present homage pays,
The Harvest early, but mature the Praise:
Great Friend of LIBERTY! in *Kings* a Name
Above all Greek, above all Roman Fame:
Whose Word is Truth, as sacred and rever'd,
As Heav'n's own Oracles from Altars heard.
Wonder of Kings! like whom, to mortal eyes
None e'er has risen, and none e'er shall rise.
  Just in one instance, be it yet confest
Your People, Sir, are partial in the rest:
Foes to all living worth except your own,
And Advocates for folly dead and gone.
Authors, like coins, grow dear as they grow old;
It is the rust we value, not the gold.
Chaucer's worst ribaldry is learn'd by rote,
And beastly Skelton Heads of Houses quote:
One likes no language but the Faery Queen;
A Scot will fight for Christ's Kirk o' the Green;
And each true Briton is to Ben so civil,
He swears the Muses met him at the Devil.
  Tho' justly Greece her eldest sons admires,
Why should not We be wiser than our Sires?
In ev'ry Public Virtue we excell;
We build, we paint, we sing, we dance as well,
And learned Athens to our Art must stoop,
Could she behold us tumbling thro' a hoop.

If Time improve our Wit as well as Wine,
Say at what age a Poet grows divine?
Shall we, or shall we not, account him so,
Who dy'd, perhaps, an hundred years ago?
End all dispute; and fix the year precise
When British bards begin t' immortalize.
'Who lasts a century can have no flaw,
'I hold that Wit a Classic, good in law.'
Suppose he wants a year, will you compound?
And shall we deem him Ancient, right and sound,
Or damn to all eternity at once,
At ninety nine, a Modern and a Dunce?
'We shall not quarrel for a year or two;
'By courtesy of England, he may do.'
Then, by the rule that made the Horse-tail bare,
I pluck out year by year, as hair by hair,
And melt down Ancients like a heap of snow:
While you, to measure merits, look in Stowe,
And estimating Authors by the year,
Bestow a Garland only on a Bier.
Shakespear (whom you and ev'ry Play-house bill
Style the divine, the matchless, what you will)
For gain, not glory, wing'd his roving flight,
And grew Immortal in his own despight.
Ben, old and poor, as little seem'd to heed
The Life to come, in ev'ry Poet's Creed.
Who now reads Cowley? if he pleases yet,
His moral pleases, not his pointed wit;
Forgot his Epic, nay Pindaric Art,
But still I love the language of his Heart.
'Yet surely, surely, these were famous men!
'What boy but hears the sayings of old Ben?
'In all debates where Critics bear a part,
'Not one but nods, and talks of Johnson's Art,

'Of Shakespear's Nature, and of Cowley's Wit;
'How Beaumont's Judgment check'd what Fletcher writ;
'How Shadwell hasty, Wycherly was slow;
'But, for the Passions, Southern sure and Rowe.
'These, only these, support the crouded stage,
'From eldest Heywood down to Cibber's age.'
All this may be; the People's Voice is odd,
It is, and it is not, the voice of God.
To Gammer Gurton if it give the bays,
And yet deny the Careless Husband praise,
Or say our Fathers never broke a rule;
Why then, I say, the Public is a fool.
But let them own, that greater Faults than we
They had, and greater Virtues, I'll agree.
Spenser himself affects the obsolete,
And Sydney's verse halts ill on Roman feet:
Milton's strong pinion now not Heav'n can bound,
Now serpent-like, in prose he sweeps the ground,
In Quibbles, Angel and Archangel join,
And God the Father turns a School-Divine.
Not that I'd lop the Beauties from his book,
Like slashing Bentley with his desp'rate Hook,
Or damn all Shakespear, like th' affected fool
At Court, who hates whate'er he read at School.
But for the Wits of either Charles's days,
The Mob of Gentlemen who wrote with Ease;
Sprat, Carew, Sedley, and a hundred more,
(Like twinkling Stars the Miscellanies o'er)
One Simile, that solitary shines
In the dry desert of a thousand lines,
Or lengthen'd Thought that gleams through many a page,
Has sanctify'd whole poems for an age.
I lose my patience, and I own it too,
When works are censur'd, not as bad, but new;

While if our Elders break all Reason's laws,
These fools demand not Pardon, but Applause.
  On Avon's bank, where flow'rs eternal blow,
If I but ask, if any weed can grow?
One Tragic sentence if I dare deride
Which Betterton's grave action dignify'd,
Or well-mouth'd Booth with emphasis proclaims,
(Tho' but, perhaps, a muster-roll of Names)
How will our Fathers rise up in a rage,
And swear, all shame is lost in George's Age!
You'd think no Fools disgrac'd the former reign,
Did not some grave Examples yet remain,
Who scorn a Lad should teach his father skill,
And, having once been wrong, will be so still.
He, who to seem more deep than you or I,
Extols old Bards, or Merlin's Prophecy,
Mistake him not; he envies, not admires,
And to debase the Sons, exalts the Sires.
Had ancient times conspir'd to dis-allow
What then was new, what had been ancient now?
Or what remain'd, so worthy to be read
By learned Critics, of the mighty Dead?
  In Days of Ease, when now the weary Sword
Was sheath'd, and *Luxury* with *Charles* restor'd;
In ev'ry Taste of foreign Courts improv'd,
'All, by the King's Example, liv'd and lov'd.'
Then Peers grew proud in Horsemanship t' excell,
New-market's Glory rose, as Britain's fell;
The Soldier breath'd the Gallantries of France,
And ev'ry flow'ry Courtier writ Romance.
Then Marble, soften'd into life, grew warm,
And yielding Metal flow'd to human form:
Lely on animated Canvas stole
The sleepy Eye, that spoke the melting soul.

No wonder then, when all was Love and Sport,
The willing Muses were debauch'd at Court:
On each enervate string they taught the note
To pant, or tremble thro' an Eunuch's throat.
  But Britain, changeful as a Child at play,
Now calls in Princes, and now turns away.
Now Whig, now Tory, what we lov'd we hate;
Now all for Pleasure, now for Church and State;
Now for Prerogative, and now for Laws;
Effects unhappy! from a Noble Cause.
  Time was, a sober Englishman wou'd knock
His servants up, and rise by five o'clock,
Instruct his Family in ev'ry rule,
And send his Wife to church, his Son to school.
To worship like his Fathers, was his care;
To teach their frugal Virtues to his Heir;
To prove, that Luxury could never hold;
And place, on good Security, his Gold.
Now times are chang'd, and one Poetic Itch
Has seiz'd the Court and City, Poor and Rich:
Sons, Sires, and Grandsires, all will wear the Bays,
Our Wives read Milton, and our Daughters Plays,
To Theatres, and to Rehearsals throng,
And all our Grace at Table is a Song.
I, who so oft renounce the Muses, lye,
Not ——'s self e'er tells more *Fibs* than I;
When, sick of Muse, our follies we deplore,
And promise our best Friends to rhyme no more;
We wake next morning in a raging fit,
And call for pen and ink to show our Wit.
  He serv'd a 'Prenticeship, who sets up shop;
Ward try'd on Puppies, and the Poor, his Drop;
Ev'n Radcliff's Doctors travel first to France,
Nor dare to practise till they've learn'd to dance.

Who builds a Bridge that never drove a pile?
(Should Ripley venture, all the world would smile)
But those who cannot write, and those who can,
All rhyme, and scrawl, and scribble, to a man.
  Yet, Sir, reflect, the mischief is not great;
These Madmen never hurt the Church or State:
Sometimes the Folly benefits mankind;
And rarely Av'rice taints the tuneful mind.
Allow him but his plaything of a Pen,
He ne'er rebels, or plots, like other men:
Flight of Cashiers, or Mobs, he'll never mind;
And knows no losses while the Muse is kind.
To cheat a Friend, or Ward, he leaves to Peter;
The good man heaps up nothing but mere metre,
Enjoys his Garden and his Book in quiet;
And then—a perfect Hermit in his diet.
  Of little use the Man you may suppose,
Who says in verse what others say in prose;
Yet let me show, a Poet 's of some weight,
And (tho' no Soldier) useful to the State.
What will a Child learn sooner than a song?
What better teach a Foreigner the tongue?
What 's long or short, each accent where to place,
And speak in public with some sort of grace.
I scarce can think him such a worthless thing,
Unless he praise some monster of a King;
Or Virtue, or Religion turn to sport,
To please a lewd, or unbelieving Court.
Unhappy Dryden!—In all Charles's days,
Roscommon only boasts unspotted bays;
And in our own (excuse some Courtly stains)
No whiter page than Addison remains.
He, from the taste obscene reclaims our Youth,
And sets the Passions on the side of Truth,

Forms the soft bosom with the gentlest art,
And pours each human Virtue in the heart.
Let Ireland tell, how Wit upheld her cause,
Her Trade supported, and supplied her Laws;
And leave on Swift this grateful verse ingrav'd,
The Rights a Court attack'd, a Poet sav'd.
Behold the hand that wrought a Nation's cure,
Stretch'd to relieve the Idiot and the Poor,
Proud Vice to brand, or injur'd Worth adorn,
And stretch the Ray to Ages yet unborn.
Not but there are, who merit other palms;
Hopkins and Sternhold glad the heart with Psalms:
The Boys and Girls whom charity maintains,
Implore your help in these pathetic strains:
How could Devotion touch the country pews,
Unless the Gods bestow'd a proper Muse?
Verse chears their leisure, Verse assists their work,
Verse prays for Peace, or sings down Pope and Turk.
The silenc'd Preacher yields to potent strain,
And feels that grace his pray'r besought in vain;
The blessing thrills thro' all the lab'ring throng,
And Heav'n is won by violence of Song.
  Our rural Ancestors, with little blest,
Patient of labour when the end was rest,
Indulg'd the day that hous'd their annual grain,
With feasts, and off'rings, and a thankful strain:
The joy their wives, their sons, and servants share,
Ease of their toil, and part'ners of their care:
The laugh, the jest, attendants on the bowl,
Smooth'd ev'ry brow, and open'd ev'ry soul:
With growing years the pleasing Licence grew,
And Taunts alternate innocently flew.
But Times corrupt, and Nature, ill-inclin'd,
Produc'd the point that left a sting behind;

Till friend with friend, and families at strife,
Triumphant Malice rag'd thro' private life.
Who felt the wrong, or fear'd it, took th' alarm,
Appeal'd to Law, and Justice lent her arm.
At length, by wholesome dread of statutes bound,
The Poets learn'd to please, and not to wound:
Most warp'd to Flatt'ry's side; but some, more nice,
Preserv'd the freedom, and forbore the vice.
Hence Satire rose, that just the medium hit,
And heals with Morals what it hurts with Wit.
We conquer'd France, but felt our captive's charms;
Her Arts victorious triumph'd o'er our Arms;
Britain to soft refinements less a foe,
Wit grew polite, and Numbers learn'd to flow.
Waller was smooth; but Dryden taught to join
The varying verse, the full resounding line,
The long majestic march, and energy divine.
Tho' still some traces of our rustic vein
And splay-foot verse, remain'd, and will remain.
Late, very late, correctness grew our care,
When the tir'd nation breath'd from civil war.
Exact Racine, and Corneille's noble fire,
Show'd us that France had something to admire.
Not but the Tragic spirit was our own,
And full in Shakespear, fair in Otway shone:
But Otway fail'd to polish or refine,
And fluent Shakespear scarce effac'd a line.
Ev'n copious Dryden wanted, or forgot,
The last and greatest Art, the Art to blot.
Some doubt, if equal pains or equal fire
The humbler Muse of Comedy require.
But in known Images of life, I guess
The labour greater, as th' indulgence less.
Observe how seldom ev'n the best succeed:

Tell me if Congreve's Fools are Fools indeed?
What pert, low Dialogue has Farqu'ar writ!
How Van wants grace, who never wanted wit!
The stage how loosely does Astræa tread,
Who fairly puts all Characters to bed:
And idle Cibber, how he breaks the laws,
To make poor Pinky eat with vast applause!
But fill their purse, our Poet's work is done,
Alike to them, by Pathos or by Pun.
  O you! whom Vanity's light bark conveys
On Fame's mad voyage by the wind of Praise,
With what a shifting gale your course you ply,
For ever sunk too low, or born too high!
Who pants for glory finds but short repose,
A breath revives him, or a breath o'erthrows.
Farewell the stage! if just as thrives the play,
The silly bard grows fat, or falls away.
  There still remains, to mortify a Wit,
The many-headed Monster of the Pit:
A senseless, worthless, and unhonour'd crowd;
Who, to disturb their betters mighty proud,
Clatt'ring their sticks before ten lines are spoke,
Call for the Farce, the Bear, or the Black-joke.
What dear delight to Britons Farce affords!
Ever the taste of Mobs, but now of Lords;
(Taste, that eternal wanderer, which flies
From heads to ears, and now from ears to eyes.)
The Play stands still; damn action and discourse,
Back fly the scenes, and enter foot and horse;
Pageants on pageants, in long order drawn,
Peers, Heralds, Bishops, Ermin, Gold, and Lawn;
The Champion too! and, to complete the jest,
Old Edward's Armour beams on Cibber's breast.
With laughter sure Democritus had dy'd,

Had he beheld an Audience gape so wide.
Let Bear or Elephant be e'er so white,
The people, sure, the people are the sight!
Ah luckless Poet! stretch thy lungs and roar,
That Bear or Elephant shall heed thee more;
While all its throats the Gallery extends,
And all the Thunder of the Pit ascends!
Loud as the Wolves on Orcas' stormy steep,
Howl to the roarings of the Northern deep.
Such is the shout, the long-applauding note,
At Quin's high plume, or Oldfield's petticoat;
Or when from Court a birth-day suit bestow'd,
Sinks the lost Actor in the tawdry load.
Booth enters—hark! the Universal Peal!
'But has he spoken?' Not a syllable.
'What shook the stage, and made the people stare?'
Cato's long Wig, flow'r'd gown, and lacquer'd chair.
  Yet lest you think I railly more than teach,
Or praise malignly Arts I cannot reach,
Let me for once presume t' instruct the times,
To know the Poet from the Man of Rhymes:
'Tis he, who gives my breast a thousand pains,
Can make me feel each Passion that he feigns;
Inrage, compose, with more than magic Art,
With Pity, and with Terror, tear my heart;
And snatch me, o'er the earth, or thro' the air,
To Thebes, to Athens, when he will, and where.
  But not this part of the poetic state
Alone, deserves the favour of the Great:
Think of those Authors, Sir, who would rely
More on a Reader's sense, than Gazer's eye.
Or who shall wander where the Muses sing?
Who climb their mountain, or who taste their spring?
How shall we fill a Library with Wit,

When Merlin's Cave is half unfurnish'd yet?
  My Liege! why Writers little claim your thought,
I guess; and, with their leave, will tell the fault:
We Poets are (upon a Poet's word)
Of all mankind, the creatures most absurd:
The season, when to come, and when to go,
To sing, or cease to sing, we never know;
And if we will recite nine hours in ten,
You lose your patience, just like other men.
Then too we hurt ourselves, when to defend
A single verse, we quarrel with a friend;
Repeat unask'd; lament, the Wit 's too fine
For vulgar eyes, and point out ev'ry line.
But most, when straining with too weak a wing,
We needs will write Epistles to the King;
And from the moment we oblige the town,
Expect a place, or pension from the Crown;
Or dubb'd Historians by express command,
T' enroll your triumphs o'er the seas and land,
Be call'd to Court to plan some work divine,
As once for Louis, Boileau and Racine.
  Yet think, great Sir! (so many Virtues shown)
Ah think, what Poet best may make them known?
Or chuse at least some Minister of Grace,
Fit to bestow the Laureat's weighty place.
  Charles, to late times to be transmitted fair,
Assign'd his figure to Bernini's care;
And great Nassau to Kneller's hand decreed
To fix him graceful on the bounding Steed;
So well in paint and stone they judg'd of merit:
But Kings in Wit may want discerning Spirit.
The Hero William, and the Martyr Charles,
One knighted Blackmore, and one pension'd Quarles;
Which made old Ben, and surly Dennis swear,

'No Lord's anointed, but a Russian Bear.'
  Not with such majesty, such bold relief,
The Forms august of King, or conqu'ring Chief,
E'er swell'd on marble; as in verse have shin'd
(In polish'd verse) the Manners and the Mind.
Oh! could I mount on the Mæonian wing,
Your Arms, your Actions, your Repose to sing!
What seas you travers'd, and what fields you fought!
Your Country's Peace, how oft, how dearly bought!
How barb'rous rage subsided at your word,
And Nations wonder'd while they dropp'd the sword!
How, when you nodded, o'er the land and deep,
Peace stole her wing, and wrapt the world in sleep;
'Till Earth's extremes your mediation own,
And Asia's Tyrants tremble at your Throne—
But Verse, alas! your Majesty disdains;
And I'm not us'd to Panegyric strains:
The Zeal of Fools offends at any time,
But most of all, the Zeal of Fools in rhyme.
Besides, a fate attends on all I write,
That when I aim at praise, they say I bite.
A vile Encomium doubly ridicules;
There 's nothing blackens like the ink of fools.
If true, a woful likeness; and if lyes,
'Praise undeserv'd is scandal in disguise:'
Well may he blush, who gives it, or receives;
And when I flatter, let my dirty leaves
(Like Journals, Odes, and such forgotten things
As Eusden, Philips, Settle, writ of Kings)
Cloath spice, line trunks, or flutt'ring in a row,
Befringe the rails of Bedlam and Soho.

One Thousand Seven Hundred and Thirty Eight

Dialogue II

1738

Afterwards called
Epilogue to the Satires

Dialogue II, lines 197–227

Ask you what Provocation I have had?
The strong Antipathy of Good to Bad.
When Truth or Virtue an Affront endures,
Th' Affront is mine, my Friend, and should be yours.
Mine, as a Foe profess'd to false Pretence,
Who think a Coxcomb's Honour like his Sense;
Mine, as a Friend to ev'ry worthy mind;
And mine as Man, who feel for all mankind.
F. You're strangely proud.
P. So proud, I am no Slave:
So impudent, I own myself no Knave:
So odd, my Country's Ruin makes me grave.
Yes, I am proud; I must be proud to see
Men not afraid of God, afraid of me:
Safe from the Bar, the Pulpit, and the Throne,
Yet touch'd and sham'd by *Ridicule* alone.
O sacred Weapon! left for Truth's defence,
Sole Dread of Folly, Vice, and Insolence!
To all but Heav'n-directed hands deny'd,
The Muse may give thee, but the Gods must guide:
Rev'rent I touch thee! but with honest zeal;
To rouse the Watchmen of the Public Weal,

To Virtue's work provoke the tardy Hall,
And goad the Prelate slumb'ring in his Stall.
  Ye tinsel Insects! whom a Court maintains,
That counts your Beauties only by your Stains,
Spin all your Cobwebs o'er the Eye of Day!
The Muse's wing shall brush you all away:
All his Grace preaches, all his Lordship sings,
All that makes Saints of Queens, and Gods of Kings.
All, all but Truth, drops dead-born from the Press,
Like the last Gazette, or the last Address.

Homer

From the Preface to *The Iliad*, 1715

HOMER is universally allow'd to have had the greatest Invention of any Writer whatever. The Praise of Judgment *Virgil* has justly contested with him, and others may have their Pretensions as to particular Excellencies; but his Invention remains yet unrival'd. Nor is it a Wonder if he has ever been acknowledg'd the greatest of Poets, who most excell'd in That which is the very Foundation of Poetry. It is the Invention that in different degrees distinguishes all great Genius's: The utmost Stretch of human Study, Learning, and Industry, which masters every thing besides, can never attain to this. It furnishes Art with all her Materials, and without it Judgment itself can at best but *steal wisely*: For Art is only like a prudent Steward that lives on managing the Riches of Nature. Whatever Praises may be given to Works of Judgment, there is not even a single Beauty in them but is owing to the Invention: As in the most regular Gardens, however Art may carry the greatest Appearance, there is not a Plant or Flower but is the Gift of Nature. The first can only reduce the Beauties of the latter into a more obvious Figure, which the common Eye may better take in, and is therefore more entertain'd with. And perhaps the reason why most Criticks are inclin'd to prefer a judicious and methodical Genius to a great and fruitful one, is, because they find it easier for themselves to pursue their Observations through an uniform and bounded Walk of Art, than to comprehend the vast and various Extent of Nature.

Our Author's Work is a wild Paradise, where if we cannot see all the Beauties so distinctly as in an order'd Garden, it is only because the Number of them is infinitely greater.

'Tis like a copious Nursery which contains the Seeds and first Productions of every kind, out of which those who follow'd him have but selected some particular Plants, each according to his Fancy, to cultivate and beautify. If some things are too luxuriant, it is owing to the Richness of the Soil; and if others are not arriv'd to Perfection or Maturity, it is only because they are over-run and opprest by those of a stronger Nature.

It is to the Strength of this amazing Invention we are to attribute that unequal'd Fire and Rapture, which is so forcible in *Homer*, that no Man of a true Poetical Spirit is Master of himself while he reads him. What he writes is of the most animated Nature imaginable; every thing moves, every thing lives, and is put in Action. If a Council be call'd, or a Battel fought, you are not coldly inform'd of what was said or done as from a third Person; the Reader is hurry'd out of himself by the Force of the Poet's Imagination, and turns in one place to a Hearer, in another to a Spectator. The Course of his Verses resembles that of the Army he describes,

Οἱ δ' ἄρ' ἴσαν, ὡσεί τε πυρὶ χθὼν πᾶσα νέμοιτο.

They pour along like a Fire that sweeps the whole Earth before it. 'Tis however remarkable that his Fancy, which is every where vigorous, is not discover'd immediately at the beginning of his Poems in its fullest Splendor: It grows in the Progress both upon himself and others, and becomes on Fire like a Chariot-Wheel, by its own Rapidity. Exact Disposition, just Thought, correct Elocution, polish'd Numbers, may have been found in a thousand; but this Poetical *Fire*, this *Vivida vis animi*, in a very few. Even in Works where all those are imperfect or neglected, this can over-power Criticism, and make us admire even while we dis-approve. Nay, where this appears, tho' attended with

Absurdities, it brightens all the Rubbish about it, 'till we see nothing but its own Splendor. This *Fire* is discern'd in *Virgil*, but discern'd as through a Glass, reflected, and more shining than warm, but every where equal and constant: In *Lucan* and *Statius*, it bursts out in sudden, short, and interrupted Flashes: In *Milton*, it glows like a Furnace kept up to an uncommon Fierceness by the Force of Art: In *Shakespear*, it strikes before we are aware, like an accidental Fire from Heaven; But in *Homer*, and in him only, it burns every where clearly, and every where irresistibly.

We acknowledge him the Father of Poetical Diction, the first who taught that *Language of the Gods* to Men. His Expression is like the colouring of some great Masters, which discovers itself to be laid on boldly, and executed with Rapidity. It is indeed the strongest and most glowing imaginable, and touch'd with the greatest Spirit. *Aristotle* had reason to say, He was the only Poet who had found out *Living Words*; there are in him more daring Figures and Metaphors than in any good Author whatever. An Arrow is *impatient* to be on the Wing, a Weapon *thirsts* to drink the Blood of an Enemy, and the like. Yet his Expression is never too big for the Sense, but justly great in proportion to it: 'Tis the Sentiment that swells and fills out the Diction, which rises with it, and forms itself about it. For in the same degree that a *Thought* is warmer, an *Expression* will be brighter; and as That is more strong, This will become more perspicuous: Like Glass in the Furnace which grows to a greater Magnitude, and refines to a greater Clearness, only as the *Breath* within is more powerful, and the *Heat* more intense.

No Author or Man ever excell'd all the World in more than one Faculty, and as *Homer* has done this in Invention,

Virgil has in Judgment. Not that we are to think *Homer* wanted Judgment, because Virgil had it in a more eminent degree; or that *Virgil* wanted Invention, because *Homer* possest a larger share of it: Each of these great Authors had more of both than perhaps any Man besides, and are only said to have less in Comparison with one another. *Homer* was the greater Genius, *Virgil* the better Artist. In one we most admire the *Man*, in the other the *Work*. *Homer* hurries and transports us with a commanding Impetuosity, *Virgil* leads us with an attractive Majesty: *Homer* scatters with a generous Profusion, *Virgil* bestows with a careful Magnificence: *Homer*, like the *Nile*, pours out his Riches with a sudden Overflow; *Virgil* like a River in its Banks, with a gentle and constant Stream. When we behold their Battels, methinks the two Poets resemble the Heroes they celebrate: *Homer*, boundless and irresistible as *Achilles*, bears all before him, and shines more and more as the Tumult increases; *Virgil*, calmly daring like *Æneas*, appears undisturb'd in the midst of the Action, disposes all about him, and conquers with Tranquillity: And when we look upon their Machines, *Homer* seems like his own *Jupiter* in his Terrors, shaking *Olympus*, scattering the Lightnings, and firing the Heavens; *Virgil*, like the same Power in his Benevolence, counselling with the Gods, laying Plans for Empires, and regularly ordering his whole Creation.

A cooler Judgment may commit fewer Faults, and be more approv'd in the Eyes of *One Sort* of Criticks: but that Warmth of Fancy will carry the loudest and most universal Applauses which holds the Heart of a Reader under the strongest Enchantment. *Homer* not only appears the Inventor of Poetry, but excells all the Inventors of other Arts in this, that he has swallow'd up the Honour of those who succeeded him. What he has done admitted no

Encrease, it only left room for Contraction or Regulation. He shew'd all the Stretch of Fancy at once; and if he has fail'd in some of his Flights, it was but because he attempted every thing. A Work of this kind seems like a mighty Tree which rises from the most vigorous Seed, is improv'd with Industry, flourishes, and produces the finest Fruit; Nature and Art have conspir'd to raise it; Pleasure and Profit join'd to make it valuable: and they who find the justest Faults, have only said, that a few Branches (which run luxuriant thro' a Richness of Nature) might be lopp'd into Form to give it a more regular Appearance.

Dedication of the Iliad

The conclusion of the Observations on the Twenty-Fourth Book

For what remains, I beg to be excus'd from the Ceremonies of taking leave at the End of my Work; and from embarassing myself, or others, with any Defences or Apologies about it. But instead of endeavouring to raise a vain Monument to my self, of the Merits or Difficulties of it (which must be left to the World, to Truth, and to Posterity) let me leave behind me a Memorial of my Friendship, with one of the most valuable Men as well as finest Writers, of my Age and Countrey: One who has try'd, and knows by his own Experience, how hard an Undertaking it is to do Justice to *Homer*: And one, who (I am sure) sincerely rejoices with me at the Period of my Labours. To Him therefore, having brought this long Work to a Conclusion, I desire to *Dedicate* it; and to have the Honour and Satisfaction of placing together, in this manner, the Names of Mr. *CONGREVE*, and of

A. POPE.

March 25.
1720.

Shakespeare

From the Preface to *The Dramatic Works of Shakespear*, 1725

IT is not my design to enter into a Criticism upon this Author; tho' to do it effectually and not superficially, would be the best occasion that any just Writer could take, to form the judgment and taste of our nation. For of all *English* Poets *Shakespear* must be confessed to be the fairest and fullest subject for Criticism, and to afford the most numerous, as well as most conspicuous instances, both of Beauties and Faults of all sorts. But this far exceeds the bounds of a Preface, the business of which is only to give an account of the fate of his Works, and the disadvantages under which they have been transmitted to us. We shall hereby extenuate many faults which are his, and clear him from the imputation of many which are not: A design, which tho' it can be no guide to future Criticks to do him justice in one way, will at least be sufficient to prevent their doing him an injustice in the other.

I cannot however but mention some of his principal and characteristic Excellencies, for which (notwithstanding his defects) he is justly and universally elevated above all other Dramatic Writers. Not that this is the proper place of praising him, but because I would not omit any occasion of doing it.

If ever any Author deserved the name of an *Original*, it was *Shakespear*. *Homer* himself drew not his art so immediately from the fountains of Nature, it proceeded thro' *Ægyptian* strainers and channels, and came to him not without some tincture of the learning, or some cast of the models, of those before him. The Poetry of *Shakespear* was Inspiration indeed: he is not so much an Imitator, as an

Instrument, of Nature; and 'tis not so just to say that he speaks from her, as that she speaks thro' him.

His *Characters* are so much Nature her self, that 'tis a sort of injury to call them by so distant a name as Copies of her. Those of other Poets have a constant resemblance, which shews that they receiv'd them from one another, and were but multiplyers of the same image: each picture like a mock-rainbow is but the reflexion of a reflexion. But every single character in *Shakespear* is as much an Individual, as those in Life itself; it is as impossible to find any two alike; and such as from their relation or affinity in any respect appear most to be Twins, will upon comparison be found remarkably distinct. To this life and variety of Character, we must add the wonderful Preservation of it; which is such throughout his plays, that had all the Speeches been printed without the very names of the Persons, I believe one might have apply'd them with certainty to every speaker.

The *Power* over our *Passions* was never possess'd in a more eminent degree, or display'd in so different instances. Yet all along, there is seen no labour, no pains to raise them; no preparation to guide our guess to the effect, or be perceiv'd to lead toward it: But the heart swells, and the tears burst out, just at the proper places: We are surpriz'd, the moment we weep; and yet upon reflection find the passion so just, that we shou'd be surpriz'd if we had not wept, and wept at the very moment.

How astonishing is it again, that the passions directly opposite to these, Laughter and Spleen, are no less at his command! that he is not more a master of the *Great*, than of the *Ridiculous* in human nature; of our noblest tendernesses, than of our vainest foibles; of our strongest emotions, than of our idlest sensations!

Nor does he only excell in the Passions: In the coolness

of Reflection and Reasoning he is full as admirable. His *Sentiments* are not only in general the most pertinent and judicious upon every subject; but by a talent very peculiar, something between Penetration and Felicity, he hits upon that particular point on which the bent of each argument turns, or the force of each motive depends. This is perfectly amazing, from a man of no education or experience in those great and publick scenes of life which are usually the subject of his thoughts: So that he seems to have known the world by Intuition, to have look'd thro' humane nature at one glance, and to be the only Author that gives ground for a very new opinion, That the Philosopher and even the Man of the world, may be *Born*, as well as the Poet.

It must be own'd that with all these great excellencies, he has almost as great defects; and that as he has certainly written better, so he has perhaps written worse, than any other. But I think I can in some measure account for these defects, from several causes and accidents; without which it is hard to imagine that so large and so enlighten'd a mind could ever have been susceptible of them. That all these Contingencies should unite to his disadvantage seems to me almost as singularly unlucky, as that so many various (nay contrary) Talents should meet in one man, was happy and extraordinary.

It must be allowed that Stage-Poetry of all other, is more particularly levell'd to please the *Populace*, and its success more immediately depending upon the *Common Suffrage*. One cannot therefore wonder, if *Shakespear* having at his first appearance no other aim in his writings than to procure a subsistance, directed his endeavours solely to hit the taste and humour that then prevailed. The Audience was generally composed of the meaner sort of people; and therefore the Images of Life were to be drawn from those of their own rank: accordingly we find, that not our Author's only but almost all the old Comedies have their Scene among *Tradesmen* and *Mechanicks*: And even their Historical Plays strictly follow the common *Old Stories* or *Vulgar Traditions* of that kind of people. In Tragedy, nothing was so sure to *Surprize* and cause *Admiration*, as the most strange, unexpected, and consequently most unnatural, Events and Incidents; the most exaggerated Thoughts; the most verbose and bombast Expression; the most pompous Rhymes, and thundering Versification. In Comedy, nothing was so sure to *please*, as mean buffoonry, vile ribaldry, and unmannerly jests of fools and clowns. Yet even in these, our Author's Wit buoys up, and is born above his subject: his Genius in those low parts is like some Prince of a Romance in the disguise of a Shepherd or Peasant; a certain Greatness and Spirit now and then break out, which manifest his higher extraction and qualities.

I will conclude by saying of *Shakespear*, that with all his faults, and with all the irregularity of his *Drama*, one may look upon his works, in comparison of those that are more finish'd and regular, as upon an ancient majestick piece of *Gothick* Architecture, compar'd with a neat Modern building: The latter is more elegant and glaring, but the former is more strong and more solemn. It must be allow'd, that in one of these there are materials enough to make many of the other. It has much the greater variety, and much the nobler apartments; tho' we are often conducted to them by dark, odd, and uncouth passages. Nor does the Whole fail to strike us with greater reverence, tho' many of the Parts are childish, ill-plac'd, and unequal to its grandeur.

NOTES

JOHNSON'S LIFE

PAGE **3,** l. 30. Joseph Spence reports that Pope said, 'I learned versification wholly from Dryden's works; who had improved it much beyond any of our former poets; and would, probably, have brought it to its perfection, had not he been unhappily obliged to write so often in haste.' (Spence's *Anecdotes*, ed. Singer, 1820, p. 281.)

PAGE **4,** l. 24. *For this reason,* &c.: 'my *Essay on Criticism* was written in 1709, and published in 1711; which is as little time as ever I let any thing of mine lay by me.' (Spence, *op. cit.*, p. 170.)

l. 28. *the two satires of Thirty-eight* (afterwards called *Epilogue to the Satires.* Dialogue I and II) were published in May and July 1738, the first by T. Cooper, the second by R. Dodsley. See pp. 143–4 and note. Robert Dodsley (1703–64) published Johnson's *London* on the same day as Dialogue I appeared. He is best known by his *Collection of Old Plays* (1st ed. 1744) and *Collection of Poems by Several Hands* (3 vols. 1748; 6 vols. 1758).

l. 34. *His declaration,* &c. Pope, in *The Guardian,* April 27, 1713, No. 40, writing anonymously, described himself as 'that Gentleman, whose Character it is, that he takes the greatest Care of his Works before they are published, and has the least Concern for them afterwards'.

PAGE **5,** l. 12. *whose education was more scholastic.* Dryden was educated at Westminster School under Dr. Busby and at Trinity College, Cambridge. Pope, owing to his religion, could not have proceeded either to a public school or to a university. But 'Mr. Pope thought himself the better, in some respects, for not having had a regular education.—He, (as he observed in particular), read originally for the sense; whereas we are taught, for so many years, to read only for words.' (Spence, *op. cit.*, pp. 279–80.)

PAGE **7,** l. 9. *traveller in the Alps*: *Essay on Criticism,* ll. 225–33; see p. 33.

l. 23. *Perrault,* Charles (1628–1703), author of *Parallèles des Anciens et des Modernes* (1688–97), in which he asserted the claims of the Moderns against the Ancients.

ll. 23–4. His phrase 'comparaisons à longue queuë' will be found in the fourth Dialogue, ed. 1693, p. 42. Addison, in *The Spectator,* No. 303, Feb. 16, 1712, made it known in England:

'Monsieur *Perrault* . . . has endeavoured to turn into Ridicule several of *Homer's* Similitudes, which he calls *Comparaisons à longue queue, Long-tailed Comparisons*.'

l. 25. *ship-race . . . chariot-race*. See *Aen*. v. 144 sqq.

l. 28. *greyhound . . . hare*. See Ovid, *Met*. i. 533 sqq.

PAGE **8,** l. 9. *Warburton*, William (1698–1779), one of Pope's chief friends during the last six years of his life and his literary executor after his death. This friendship coincides with Pope's intellectual and, perhaps, personal reaction against Bolingbroke. Warburton was made Bishop of Gloucester in 1759. His edition of Pope's works (9 volumes, 1751) has provided the basis of most modern texts.

PAGE **10,** l. 1. *curiosa felicitas*, i.e. 'careful or laboured happiness', used by Petronius Arbiter (113. 5) of Horace. Cf. *Essay on Criticism*, l. 142: 'For there's a happiness as well as care.'

PAGE **13,** l. 33. *Boileau*, Nicolas Boileau, Sieur Despréaux (1637–1711), French poet and critic, author of *Le Lutrin* (1674–83), the principal mock-heroic poem in French, and *L'Art poétique*. See prefatory note to *The Rape of the Lock*.

PAGE **14,** l. 4. *Swift's remonstrances*. In his letter to Pope, June 28, 1715, Swift says: 'I borrowed your Homer . . . yet I am angry at some bad rhymes and triplets, and pray in your next do not let me have so many unjustifiable rhymes to *war* and *gods*.' (*Correspondence of Swift*, ed. Elrington Ball, vol. ii, p. 287.)

l. 7. *Swift's edict*. See Swift's letter to Thomas Beach, April 12, 1735, '. . . a triplet, which was a vicious way of rhyming, wherewith Dryden abounded, and was imitated by all the bad versifiers in Charles the Second's reign. . . . I was so angry at these corruptions, that above twenty-four years ago I banished them all by one triplet, with the Alexandrine, upon a very ridiculous subject. I absolutely did prevail with Mr. Pope, and Gay, and Dr. Young, and one or two more, to reject them. Mr. Pope never used them till he translated Homer, which was too long a work to be so very exact in; and I think in one or two of his last poems he hath, out of laziness, done the same thing, though very seldom.' (*Correspondence*, vol. v, p. 162.)

l. 9. *Fenton*, Elijah (1683–1730), one of Pope's principal collaborators in his *Odyssey*. See Johnson's *Life* for an amusing account of his indolent habits.

l. 11. *Watts*, Isaac (1674–1748), author of many famous hymns. The reference here is to his *Improvement of the Mind* (1741). 'Few books', says Johnson in his Life of Watts, 'have been perused by me with greater pleasure.'

ll. 18–19. *Hall's Satires*. Joseph Hall (1574–1656), bishop of Exeter and Norwich, claimed to be the father of English satire:

'I first adventure; follow me who list
And be the second English satirist.'

(*Virgidemiarum* (1597) Prologue ll. 3–4.)

HAZLITT'S LECTURE, ETC.

PAGE **17,** l. 1. *The question, whether Pope was a poet*; cf. Johnson, pp. 14–15.

PAGE **19,** ll. 32–4. *More subtle web,* &c. *Faerie Queene,* II. xii. 77.

PAGE **20,** l. 16. *character of Addison*; see pp. 121–2 and note.

l. 19. *Buckingham*; see p. 103 and note.

ll. 30–1. *Epistle to Jervas,* first printed at the beginning of an edition of Dryden's translation of Du Fresnoy's *Art of Painting,* 1716. Charles Jervas (1675–1739), a fashionable portrait-painter, was a pupil of Sir Godfrey Kneller. Pope took lessons from him in painting. A conceited, fussy individual, he has left us attractive portraits of Pope and Swift.

PAGE **21,** l. 9. *Zeuxis' Helen.* A picture of Helen was painted by Zeuxis, one of the greatest painters of antiquity, for the temple of Hera at Croton, probably at the end of the fourth century B.C. Elizabeth, Countess of Bridgewater, was the third daughter of the Duke of Marlborough.

l. 10. *Granville's Myra.* George Granville (1666–1735) was created in 1711 Lord Lansdowne of Bideford. See note on p. 120, l. 135, and the introductory note to the *Essay on Criticism.* 'Myra' was the poetical name which he gave to the Countess of Newburgh, to whom he addressed many of his poems.

l. 23. *Et quum conabar scribere, versus erat.* The accepted reading is 'Et quod tentabam dicere, versus erat'. Ovid, *Tristia,* IV. x. 26.

l. 32. *Atterbury,* Francis (1663–1732), was a High Church leader, Dean of Carlisle 1704, and Bishop of Rochester 1713. His strong Jacobite sympathies led to his banishment in 1723. Like Oxford and Bolingbroke, he had been a member of the Scriblerus Club.

PAGE **22,** l. 1. *Ayrton,* William (1777–1858), musical critic, was a well-known figure at the Lambs' Thursday evening parties; he was called by Hazlitt 'the Will Honeycomb of our set'.

l. 13. *Despise low joys.* Imitation of Horace, *Sixth Epistle, Book I,* ll. 60–3. Lord Cornbury (1710–53), heir to the Earl of Clarendon, is said to have refused a pension.

ll. 20 sqq. *Conspicuous scene,* ibid., ll. 50–4. William Murray (1705–93), to whom Pope dedicated this poem, became Chief Justice of the King's Bench and was created Earl of Mansfield. Hyde is the great Earl of Clarendon, the minister of Charles II.

ll. 26–7. *Why rail they then,* from *One Thousand Seven Hundred and Thirty Eight; Dialogue* II, ll. 138–9. Henry St. John (1678–1751), created Viscount Bolingbroke in 1712, was the most able and energetic member of Queen Anne's last ministry, and the intimate friend of Pope and Swift. His influence on Pope is perhaps clearest in the *Essay on Man,* but Pope told Spence that he suggested to him his Horatian imitations. (Spence, *Anecdotes,* p. 297.)

l. 30. *But why then publish,* from *Epistle to Arbuthnot,* ll. 135–46; see p. 120 and notes.

Campbell's Essay

Page **25,** ll. 8 sqq. *Satan's spear.* See *Paradise Lost,* i. 281 sqq.

l. 11. *Tuscan artist,* Galileo.

ll. 12 sqq. *spirit-stirring drum.* See *Othello,* Act iii, sc. iii, ll. 352–4.

ll. 16 sqq. *the cloud-capt towers.* See *The Tempest,* Act iv, sc. i, ll. 152–3.

Page **26,** ll. 6–7. *Builds life on death,* &c.: *Moral Essays,* Epistle iii, 'Of the Use of Riches', ll. 167–8.

ll. 16–17. *qualem vix repperit,* &c.; Ausonius xxx. 1–2. Decius Magnus Ausonius (310–90), of Burdigala (Bordeaux), the chief Latin poet of the fourth century.

De Quincey on Pope

Page **29,** ll. 25–6. *Once* (*like herself*). See p. 82, ll. 311–12. For the other lines quoted, see pp. 82, 83.

Ode on Solitude

Page **32.** This poem was said by Pope to have been written when he was 'not twelve years old', but he revised it before he let it be printed.—'Pope, in that production of his boyhood, the *Ode to Solitude,* and in his *Essay on Criticism,* has furnished proofs that at one period of his life he felt the charm of a sober and subdued style'—Wordsworth, letter to W. Dyce, May 10, 1830.

An Essay on Criticism

An Essay on Criticism, published anonymously in 1711, is a remarkable example of a species of poetry once fashionable. Perhaps its success is most apparent when it is compared with such poems as Mulgrave's *Essay on Satire* (?1679) and *Essay on Poetry* (1682–91), Roscommon's *Essay on Translated Verse* (1684, 1685), Granville's *Essay upon Unnatural Flights in Poetry* (1701), and Parnell's *Essay on the Different Styles of Poetry* (1713). With the publication of this piece Pope took his place amongst the notable authors of the day. (See *The Spectator*, No. 253, Dec. 20, 1711.) It argues effectively and delightfully for the validity of personal taste, while at the same time maintaining that without submission to appropriate intellectual discipline, even the best taste is misleading and capricious.

PAGE **33**, l. 216. *Pierian*, sacred to the Muses.

l. 225 sqq. See Johnson's comments on this simile, p. 7.

PAGE **34**, l. 267. *La Mancha's Knight*. The incident is found in the spurious second part of *Don Quixote* (1614), by an unknown writer who assumed the name of Alonzo Fernandez de Avellenada.

l. 270. *Dennis*, John (1657–1734), an able but irascible critic. He speaks of 'the Greatness of the Grecian Stage' in the introductory matter to his *Grounds of Criticism in Poetry* (1704). He attacked Pope and his works bitterly for a number of years, and earned a place in *The Dunciad*. In 1733, however, Pope wrote a prologue to a play performed for Dennis's benefit 'when he was old, blind, and in great distress'. See *Epistle to Arbuthnot*, ll. 370–1.

PAGE **36**, l. 328. *Fungoso*, an awkward would-be courtier in Ben Jonson's *Every Man out of his Humour*.

PAGE **37**, l. 361. *Denham*, Sir John (1615–69), won his reputation by *Cooper's Hill* (1643), which Johnson described as the first instance of 'a species of composition that may be denominated *local poetry*, of which the fundamental subject is some particular landscape to be poetically described, with the addition of such embellishments as may be supplied by historical retrospection or incidental meditation'. Pope's *Windsor-Forest* (1713) is a poem of this kind. Denham and Edmund Waller (1606–87) were associated in poetical reputation as masters of the heroic couplet. Cf. Dryden, *Essay of Dramatic Poesy*: 'nothing so even, sweet, and flowing, as Mr. Waller; nothing so majestic, so correct, as Sir John Denham' (*Essays*, ed. W. P. Ker, i. 35). See also *Epistle to Augustus*, l. 267.

l. 365. *Echo to the sense*. Cf. Roscommon's *Essay on Translated Verse*, ll. 343–4:

> '*Sublime* or *Low, Unbended* or *Intense*,
> The *Sound* is still a *Comment* to the *Sense*.'

Johnson dealt with this question in *The Rambler*, No. 92 and No. 94, *The Idler*, No. 60, and his *Life* of Pope.

l. 372. See *Aeneid*, vii. 808–11.

l. 374. *Timotheus.* See Dryden's *Alexander's Feast, or, The Power of Musique.* Timotheus, a musician of Thebes, was a favourite of Alexander the Great.

l. 376. *the son of Libyan Jove,* Alexander the Great, who claimed divine descent from Jupiter Ammon.

The Rape of the Lock

This poem, the best known and most popular that Pope wrote, first appeared in two cantos in Bernard Lintot's collection called *Miscellaneous Poems and Translations* (May 1712). Its object, more probably its excuse, was to help to compose the quarrel between the related families of Petre and Fermor caused by Lord Petre's jaunty act of ill-bred waggishness. Although Pope's effort was probably not particularly pleasing to the parties concerned, both of whom had behaved foolishly and were unlikely to welcome publicity, its appearance placed him at the head of contemporary poets. He enlarged it to five cantos and published it separately in 1714, when it sold in thousands. The chief additions in this version are the descriptions of Belinda's toilet, the game of ombre, and the cave of spleen, as well as the whole apparatus of the sylphs and gnomes. Lines 7–36 of Canto v were added in the 1717 edition of Pope's *Works*.

Despite the incessant allusions to stock passages in Homer, Virgil, Ovid, and Milton, this poem is perhaps fresher and more obviously delightful than any other work of Pope. It is in the tradition of the mock epic—that form of inverted heroic poetry of which *The Dunciad* is a more heavily charged and gravely purposeful example. Amongst its predecessors in this kind are *The Battle of the Frogs and Mice* (translated by Pope's friend Thomas Parnell), *The Game of Chess*, by Vida (from which the game of ombre episode is imitated), Boileau's *Lutrin*, and Garth's *Dispensary* (1699).

PAGE **40**, l. 26. *Le Comte de Gabalis, ou Entretiens sur les sciences secrètes*, by the Abbé de Montfaucon de Villars, was published in 1670 and translated into English in 1714, perhaps in consequence of the popularity of this poem.

PAGE **41**. *Nolueram*, &c. Martial, *Epigr.* xii. 84.

Canto I

l. 3. *Caryl.* John Caryll (1666–1736) was an intimate friend of Pope. A cousin of Lord Petre ('The Baron'), it was he who suggested to Pope the subject of the poem.

PAGE **42,** l. 23. *a Birth-night Beau,* a beau whom she would have met at a ball given on one of the royal birthdays.

l. 32. *The silver token,* silver coins put by fairies into the shoes of cleanly and industrious maids; sluts were not so favoured.

the circled green. Cf. Shakespeare's 'green-sour ringlets'. *Tempest,* V. i. 37.

PAGE **43,** l. 44. *the Ring,* where Society rode and drove in Hyde Park.

ll. 47–8. Cf. Dryden's *Flower and Leaf,* ll. 482–3:

'And all those airy Shapes you now behold
Were humane Bodies once, and cloath'd with earthly Mold.'

In *Le Comte de Gabalis* the sylphs are not metamorphosed human beings, but are made from the purest portions of the elements which they severally inhabit.

l. 56. *Ombre,* a three-handed game in which the ombre—Spanish *el hombre,* the man—played against the other two. For a description see *The Game of Ombre,* by Henry H. Gibbs, second ed. 1878.

l. 62. *elemental Tea*: elemental because made of the element—water—from which in *Le Comte de Gabalis* the nymphs were made.

ll. 69–70. Cf. *Paradise Lost,* i. 423 sqq. In *Le Comte de Gabalis* sylphs are not thus privileged.

PAGE **44,** l. 105. *thy protection claim,* claim to protect thee.

Canto II

PAGE **47,** l. 28. Cf. Dryden's translation of *Persius* (1693), Satire v, l. 247, 'Can draw you to her, *with a single Hair*'.

l. 45. 'Adapted from Virgil, *Aen.* xi. 795' (Pope's note).

PAGE **48,** l. 70. Cf. *Paradise Lost,* i. 589.

l. 73. *Sylphids,* female sylphs in *Le Comte de Gabalis.*

ll. 81–3. 'The light militia' mentioned in Canto I, l. 42.

PAGE **49,** l. 113. *Brillante* appropriately looks after her ear-rings or ear-drops, which are set with brilliants; cf. l. 140.

l. 115. *Crispissa,* apparently the sylph who was later cut in half.

l. 119. Cf. 'Clypei dominus septemplicis Aiax', Ovid, *Met.* xiii. 2. See *The Spectator,* No. 127, July 26, 1711.

PAGE **50,** l. 133. *Ixion* was punished by Zeus for ingratitude and presumption by being fastened to a perpetually revolving wheel.

Canto III

l. 3. *structure,* Hampton Court.

ll. 7, 8. *obey . . . Tea*: a perfect rhyme in Pope's day; cf. Canto I, ll. 61, 62.

PAGE **51,** l. 19. Ambrose Philips, *Pastorals*, v, ll. 7–8:

'The Sun, now mounted to the Noon of Day,
Began to shoot direct his burning Ray.'

l. 22. The fashionable hour for dinner was then 4 o'clock.

l. 30. *sacred nine*, each hand at ombre consists of nine cards.

l. 33. *Matadore*. The three best trumps were *Matadores*; these were *Spadille* (Ace of Spades), *Manille* (the lowest card of whatever suit 'ombre' named as trumps; in this particular game the 2 of Spades, Belinda having declared Spades trumps), *Basto* (ace of clubs). In a black suit the 2 was the lowest card, in a red suit the 7. The black suits had no aces as such, since these were always *Spadille* and *Basto*; in a red suit, when not trumps, the ace ranked next below the knave; when trumps, the ace ranked above the king, i.e. it was the fourth highest trump and was then known as *Punto*.

l. 45. *the skilful Nymph*. Belinda was 'ombre' and therefore declared trumps.

PAGE **52,** l. 61. *mighty Pam*, the Knave of Clubs, the highest card in the game of *loo*.

l. 67. *His warlike Amazon*. The Baron trumps Belinda's King of Clubs with his Queen of Spades—the last remaining trump. This is the fifth trick.

l. 74. The King of Clubs alone carries an orb.

ll. 75 sqq. The Baron makes three tricks with his diamonds, but his Ace of Hearts is taken by Belinda's King, which gives her the odd trick.

l. 76. The King of Diamonds is depicted in profile.

PAGE **53,** l. 92. *Codille*. 'If either of the adversaries win the game, he is said to give *Codille* to the Ombre' (H. Gibbs, *Game of Ombre*, 1878, p. 26).

l. 106. *the mill*, for grinding the coffee.

l. 107. *Altars of Japan*, lacquered trays.

l. 110. *China's earth*, the cups.

PAGE **54,** l. 122. *Scylla's Fate*. See Ovid, *Met.* viii.

l. 152. 'See Milton lib. vi of Satan cut asunder by the Angel Michael' (Pope's note).

PAGE **55,** l. 163. 'Virgil, *Eclogues*, v. 76 sqq.' (Pope's note).

l. 165. *Atalantis, Secret Memoirs and Manners of Several Persons of Quality of Both sexes. From the New Atalantis* (1709), by Mrs. Manley, a literary and social adventuress whom Swift befriended.

ll. 177–8. 'Ille quoque eversus mons est, &c.
Quid faciant crines, cum ferro talia cedant?
Catull. de com. Berenices' (Pope's note).

See Catullus, lxvi, ll. 43–7.

Canto IV

PAGE **56,** ll. 16, 20. 'The Spleen' was the fashionable name from about 1660 for a fit of depression or moroseness. See poems with this title by Anne, Countess of Winchelsea (1701) and Matthew Green (1737).

l. 24. *Megrim*, cf. French *migraine*.

l. 25. *wait*, i.e. wait upon, are in attendance on.

l. 38. *a new disease*, so that they might have another excuse for showing off their new night-dresses.

PAGE **57,** l. 43. *on rolling spires*, coiled in spirals; cf. *Paradise Lost*, ix. 501–3.

l. 46. *machines*, mechanical stage contrivances. 'Angels in machines' are supernatural persons. See Pope's Preface to the poem, p. 40.

l. 51. *Iliad*, xviii. 373–6.

l. 59. *vapours*, now called hysteria.

l. 69. *Citron-waters*, made from brandy flavoured with the rind of citron or lemon.

PAGE **58,** l. 82. See *Odyssey*, x.

l. 89. *Thalestris* was the Queen of the Amazons; the name is here given to Mrs. Morley, the sister of 'Sir Plume'.

l. 102. *loads of lead*, part of the apparatus of curl-papers.

PAGE **59,** ll. 114–15. Apparently the Baron proposed to wear Belinda's hair in a diamond ring.

l. 117. *Hyde-park Circus*. See Canto I, l. 44 and note.

l. 118. A fashionable wit would naturally live in the West End, well outside the City.

l. 121. *Sir Plume*. Probably Sir George Browne, Bart., of Caversham.

l. 124. *nice conduct of a clouded cane*. Cf. *The Tatler*, No. 103, Dec. 3–Dec. 6, 1709. Sir George 'was the only one of the Party who took the thing seriously. He was angry that the Poet should make him talk nothing but nonsense; and, in truth, one could not well blame him' (Warburton).

Canto V

PAGE **61,** ll. 7–36. Added in 1717. *Clarissa* is introduced 'to open more clearly the moral of the poem, in a parody of the speech of Sarpedon to Glaucus in Homer' (Pope's note).

l. 14. *side-box*, where the gentlemen sat; ladies sat in the 'front-box' (l. 17).

PAGE **62,** l. 60. Cf. Mulgrave's *Essay on Poetry*, l. 202: 'They *sigh* in *Simile*, and *dye* in *Rhime*.'

l. 62. *Dapperwit*, a character in Wycherley's *Love in a Wood*.

l. 63. Sir Fopling Flutter was the hero of Etherege's best play, *The Man of Mode, or Sir Fopling Flutter* (1676).

l. 64. *Those eyes are made so killing*, from a song in Act III, sc. iii of the opera *Camilla*, produced in London in 1706.

l. 65. 'Sic, ubi fata vocant, udis abiectus in herbis,
Ad vada Mæandri concinit albus olor.'
(Ovid, *Heroides*, Ep. vii, 1 sqq.)

PAGE **63**, l. 71. 'Vid. Homer, *Il.* viii and Virg. *Aen.* xii' (Pope's note).

l. 89. 'In imitation of the progress of Agamemnon's sceptre in Homer, *Iliad* ii' (Pope's note).

PAGE **64**, ll. 103–4. Cf. Dryden's *Alexander's Feast*, ll. 35, 36:
'A present deity, they shout around:
A present deity, the vaulted roofs rebound.'

ll. 115–16. *vases* . . . *cases*, a good rhyme according to current eighteenth-century pronunciation.

l. 118. *lovers hearts*. The apostrophe after 's' as a sign of the possessive plural was introduced in the eighteenth century and was not regular till the end of the century.

l. 129. *Berenice's Locks*. Berenice—sister and wife of Ptolemy III—dedicated her hair to Venus as a thank-offering for Ptolemy's victories. It was stolen from the temple and was subsequently declared to have been taken up to heaven by Jupiter who hung it amongst the stars. Callimachus, the elegiac poet, celebrated this occurrence in a poem, which was subsequently translated by Catullus (LXVI). See note on p. 55, l. 177.

l. 133. *the Mall*, on the north side of St. James's Park, a fashionable promenade in the eighteenth century.

PAGE **65**, l. 136. *Rosamonda's lake*, in the south-west corner of St. James's Park. Its neighbourhood was a popular place for assignations.

l. 137. *Partridge*, a maker of prophetic almanacks, was the subject of Swift's best-known 'bite'. Writing as Isaac Bickerstaff, in *Predictions for the year 1708*, he foretold Partridge's own death in that year. He then published an account of the fulfilment of this prophecy, and treated with humorous contempt the wretched Partridge's attempts to demonstrate his continued existence.

l. 138. *Galilæo*. This is the regular spelling of 'Galileo' in the editions of *The Rape of the Lock* published in Pope's lifetime.

TO A YOUNG LADY ON HER LEAVING THE TOWN . . .

PAGE **68**. The young lady was Miss Martha Blount of Mapledurham, a lifelong friend of Pope. The Coronation referred to is that of George I (Oct. 20, 1714).

PAGE **69,** ll. 11–12. Cf. Etherege's *The Man of Mode, or Sir Fopling Flutter,* Act v, sc. ii, ll. 421 sqq. Harriet loq. 'To a great rambling lone house, that looks as it were not inhabited, the family's so small; there you'l find my Mother, an old lame Aunt, and my self, Sir, perch'd up on Chairs at a distance in a large parlour; sitting moping like three or four Melancholy Birds in a spacious vollary—Does not this stagger your Resolution?'

l. 24. *Whisk,* old form of 'whist'.

PAGE **70,** l. 46. *Parthenissa,* the fanciful name in which Martha Blount corresponded with some of her friends; in later editions 'soft Parthenia'.

Elegy to the Memory of an Unfortunate Lady

About the year 1711 Pope took a romantic interest in the fortunes of an unhappily married lady named Mrs. Weston, who has been identified on very slight evidence with the Unfortunate Lady of the poem. Her troubles may possibly have suggested the subject to Pope, though the details of the stories have not much resemblance.

l. 14. *fault of Angels,* cf. *Henry VIII,* Act III, sc. ii:

'*Cromwel,* I charge thee, fling away Ambition,
By that sinne fell the Angels.'

Eloisa to Abelard

PAGE **73.** This poem, like the two preceding, was inspired by tenderer emotions than we usually associate with Pope's work. Written, like them, while he was also engaged in the heavier labour in which his version of the *Iliad* involved him, it is probably the last of his poems to show traces of the *Windsor Forest* atmosphere which appears so frequently in his early work. The 'ten years' during which he was 'to comment and translate' were to run out before he again attempted original work on a large scale. He then appears as the fully developed master of satire. The literary influence of his earlier groups of friends has been profoundly modified by the new direction given to his genius by his absorption of the ideals of the Scriblerus Club, and *The Dunciad* reveals him as the most formidable living poet and as Dryden's true successor and equal.

The prose basis of *Eloisa and Abelard* is to be found in John Hughes's translation from the Latin of the letters of Heloise and Abelard (1713). But Pope had already handled a similar theme in his translation of Ovid's *Sappho to Phaon* (1712).

l. 7. *From Abelard it came,* the letters of Abelard to his friend which had fallen into her hands.

PAGE **74**, l. 36. *sad variety of woe.* Cf. Dryden's *State of Innocence and Fall of Man*, Lucifer's opening speech:

'In liquid burnings, or on dry to dwell,
Is all the sad variety of hell.'

PAGE **77**, l. 133. Abelard had himself founded the Monastery of the Paraclete.

EPISTLE TO ROBERT, EARL OF OXFORD

PAGE **84**. This poem is one of the most charming of Pope's complimentary pieces.

Robert Harley (1661–1724, created Earl of Oxford and Mortimer 1711) was leader of the great Tory Ministry 1710–14. After the death of Queen Anne he was for a while imprisoned in the Tower, and spent his later years in retirement at his seat in Herefordshire. He was a capable parliamentary manager, but irritated his colleagues by his caution and secrecy; Bolingbroke in particular had no sympathy with his moderation. This moderation showed itself in a desire to placate as far as possible the less intransigent of his political enemies. A patron of letters and intimate friend both of Pope and Swift, whose correspondence abounds with charming and kindly allusions to him, he was particularly generous to Prior in his last years. He had himself taken great delight in the company of the Scriblerus Club. He formed a famous library; his manuscripts are the great Harleian collection in the British Museum.

Thomas Parnell (1679–1718) was a minor poet and the friend of Pope and Swift. At the conclusion of his notes to *The Iliad* Pope says that Parnell entrusted him 'almost with his dying breath' with the publication of his poems.

THE DUNCIAD

PAGE **88**. This is Pope's most important poem. The theme of Dulness was probably first meditated by him about 1720; and part of a poem on this subject, and perhaps with this title, had been written by 1725 (see Pope's letter to Swift of October 15, 1725). Later, under the stimulus of Lewis Theobald's *Shakespeare Restored* (1726), he developed the pedantry *motif* and recast the work on more ambitious lines. The intellectual and literary ideals of the Scriblerus Club are reflected throughout *The Dunciad*. Besides dulness and pedantry, poverty—the poverty which Pope chooses to consider the attendant of bad writing—is a main object of satire. Its sheer poetic intensity allows it to be read with pleasure—despite incessant reference to persons of small importance in their day and none at all in ours—without the help of an elaborate apparatus of notes. A detailed knowledge of contemporary writings is necessary for the fullest appreciation of Pope's art, but it is certainly possible to read at any rate Book I straight through with a good deal of enjoyment of its poetry alone. Hitherto Pope had only dabbled very slightly in personal satire; henceforth he was to be the applauded and dreaded master of satiric portraiture.

The earliest editions of the poem, in three books and with Theobald as the hero, appeared in 1728. In the following year came the official edition, *The Dunciad, Variorum. With the Prolegomena of Scriblerus*, the title-page of which is reproduced on p. 88. The fourth book was published separately in 1742 as *The New Dunciad: As it was Found In the Year* 1741, and in 1743 the final version of the whole poem, in four books with Colley Cibber as the hero, was given to the public.

Book I

This book deals with the elevation of 'Bays', i.e. Colley Cibber, who had succeeded Laurence Eusden as Poet Laureate in 1730, to the throne of the kingdom of Dulness. His reign will inaugurate the return of intellectual obscurity and confusion, the final triumph of which is the theme of Bk. IV.

PAGE **89,** l. 6. *Dunce the second . . . the first.* Cf. Dryden, *Epistle to Mr. Congreve* (1694), l. 48: 'For Tom the Second reigns like Tom the First.'

ll. 19–26. The most splendid of Pope's many tributes to Swift. Cf. *Epistle to Augustus*, ll. 221–8.

Drapier. M. B. Drapier was the title under which Swift wrote the famous *Letters* (April–December 1724) which unbound 'his grieved Country's copper chains', i.e. the 'job' by which William Wood had obtained a monopoly for providing Ireland with a copper coinage.

Bickerstaff. See note on *Rape of the Lock*, v. 137.

Cervantes and *Rabelais* represent respectively the irony and breadth of Swift's wit.

l. 25. *thy Bœotia*, i.e. Ireland, the country of Swift's ever-lamented exile.

PAGE **90,** l. 30. *Monroe* was a doctor in Bedlam. His patients are alleged to have attempted on one occasion to throw him into their soup.

l. 32. *Cibber*, Colley (1671–1757), actor-manager and dramatist, replaced Lewis Theobald as the hero of *The Dunciad* in 1743. By far his most interesting work is his *Apology for the Life of Mr. Colley Cibber, Comedian* (1740). Pope's enmity towards him is said to have dated from the failure of *Three*

Hours after Marriage (1717), a play which he wrote with John Gay and to which Cibber made slighting allusions on the stage. *A Letter from Mr. Cibber to Mr. Pope* (1742), which ridiculed Pope damagingly but not ill-humouredly, may have been the occasion for his promotion to hero. It is more likely that Cibber knew about his coming 'coronation' and got his blow in first. In 1744 he returned to the battle with *Another Occasional Letter from Mr. Cibber to Mr. Pope*. Though a poor poet Cibber was by no means ideally suited to his mock-heroic role. Pope has a friendly allusion to his *Careless Husband* in the *Epistle to Augustus*, l. 92.

l. 34. *The Cave of Poverty* is the title of a poem by Theobald published in 1715.

l. 40. *Curl* and *Lintot*, see *Epistle to Arbuthnot*, ll. 53 and 62 notes. *rubric*, see *Epistle to Arbuthnot*, l. 215 note.

l. 57. *genial Jacob*. Jacob Tonson the elder (1656–1736) is probably referred to here. He had made his name and fortune as Dryden's publisher and had printed Pope's earliest work, *Pastorals*, in his Miscellany (1709). There were three Jacob Tonsons in the publishing world of the eighteenth century, the old man, his nephew, and great-nephew.

Third day. The profits from the third day's performance of a play went to the author.

Page **91,** l. 85. * *, originally *Thorold*, the name of the Lord Mayor of London in 1720.

l. 90. *Settle's numbers*. Elkanah Settle (1648–1724), poet and playwright, was the last City Poet (1691–1724). Dryden had conferred immortality on him as Doeg in *Absalom and Achitophel*, Pt. II.

Page **92,** l. 98. *Heywood's days*. The dramatist Thomas Heywood, so much admired by Charles Lamb, had been one of the City Poets. He was referred to contemptuously by Dryden in *Mac Flecknoe*. *The Dunciad* is an elaboration and expansion of the central idea of *Mac Flecknoe*, the ceremonial and ironical crowning of a dull poet.

l. 108. *Bays's monster-breeding breast*. Bays because Cibber was Poet-Laureate; also he had played the part of Bays in *The Rehearsal* when he made a reference to the mummy and the crocodile in *Three Hours after Marriage* which infuriated Pope. See above l. 32 note.

ll. 127 sqq. Cibber adapted many old plays, English and foreign.

Page **93,** l. 140. *Quarles*, Francis Quarles (1592–1644), author of *Emblems*, 1635. The engravings by William Marshall in this book seemed to Pope to be better than the verse. Cf.

the satirical couplet on Rogers's *Italy* (*The Maclise Portrait Gallery*, ed. 1883, p. 16):

'Of Rogers's *Italy* Luttrell relates
That 'twould have been *dished*, were it not for the *plates*.'

l. 141. *Ogilby the great*, John Ogilby (1600–76), translator of Homer and Virgil in massive folios. He is satirized as a poet by Dryden as well as by Pope, but he is important in the development of English cartography.

l. 142. *Newcastle*, Margaret Cavendish (1624–74), Duchess of Newcastle, best known now by her *Life* of her husband and her autobiography. She is the 'somewhat fantastical, and original-brain'd, generous Margaret Newcastle' of Charles Lamb's essay on Mackery End.

l. 146. *Settle*. See l. 90.

Banks, John Banks, a minor dramatist, author of *The Unhappy Favourite, or the Earl of Essex* and *Vertue Betray'd or Anna Bullen* (both 1682).

Broome. William Broome (1689–1745), one of Pope's collaborators in his translation of the *Odyssey*, might be referred to here; but Pope and Warburton have a note (1743) which declares that the reference is to 'a serving man of Ben Jonson', i.e. Richard Broome (*ob. c.* 1652) the dramatist.

ll. 147 sqq. These lines were appropriate enough in the original version of the poem when Theobald was the hero, but no suggestion of pedantry or antiquarianism could attach to Cibber.

l. 149. *Wynkyn*, Wynkyn de Worde, Caxton's successor.

l. 153. *De Lyra*. Nicholas of Lyra (*c.* 1265–1349) was a voluminous commentator on the whole Bible. His *Postilla literalis* (1322–31) and *Postilla mystica seu moralis* (1339) were well known in the fourteenth and fifteenth centuries. His principal works were first printed—in weighty folios—between 1471–83.

l. 154. *Philemon*, Philemon Holland (1552–1637), the greatest of the Elizabethan classical translators.

ll. 155 sqq. Cf. *The Rape of the Lock*, ii. 35 sqq.

PAGE **94,** l. 167. *Sir Fopling's Periwig*. See *The Rape of the Lock*, v. 63 note.

l. 188. *once betray'd me into common sense*, presumably a reference to *The Careless Husband*; see *Epistle to Augustus*, l. 92.

PAGE **95,** l. 203. *White's*. Cibber was a frequenter of White's. Cf. *Tatler*, No. 1. 'All accounts of Gallantry, Pleasure, and Entertainment, shall be under the Article of White's Chocolate-house.' *Doctors* are loaded dice.

l. 208. *Ridpath* and *Mist*, respectively Whig and Tory journalists.

l. 216. *Ralph*, James (?1705–62), hack writer and journalist. He attacked Pope in *Sawney*, for which he was placed in *The Dunciad* of 1729. Pope had not mentioned him earlier.

Henly, John (1692–1756), 'Orator Henley', a well-known preacher who styled himself 'the Restorer of ancient eloquence', and wrote for Walpole.

l. 222. *Hockley-hole* was famous for its bear-baitings, bull-baitings, and prize-fights, which were attended by all classes.

l. 231. *gratis-given Bland.* Writings in support of Walpole's government were sometimes distributed to different parts of the country free. Henry Bland, a scholar who wrote for *The Daily Gazetteer*, Walpole's chief paper, was Dean of Durham from 1728 to 1746 and Provost of Eton from 1732 to 1746.

PAGE **96,** l. 233. *Ward.* Edward Ward's best-known work to-day is *The London Spy* (1698–1703). He attacked Pope particularly in *Durgen* and *Apollo's Maggot in his Cups* (both printed in 1729). An inn-keeper, he was once pilloried for the intemperate expression of his Tory opinions in *Hudibras Redivivus* (1705).

l. 234. *Mundungus*, bad tobacco. The suggestion is that Ward's poems were used to pack up this tobacco when exported.

l. 238. *Tate*, Nahum Tate (1652–1715), who succeeded Shadwell as Poet Laureate in 1692.

l. 240. *Shadwell*, Thomas Shadwell (1642–92), the hero of *Mac Flecknoe* and Og in *Absalom and Achitophel.* He succeeded Dryden as Poet Laureate on the accession of William III.

l. 265. *wait*, attend; cf. *The Rape of the Lock*, iv. 25.

PAGE **97,** l. 270. *Quidnuncs*, news-hunters.

l. 280. *the eel of science.* Cf. Swift, *A Tale of a Tub*, Sect. vii: '... the Index, by which the whole Book is governed and turned, like Fishes by the Tail.'

ll. 285–6. See ll. 127 sqq. and note. Tibbald (i.e. Lewis Theobald), in addition to editing Shakespeare, adapted *Richard II* (1720), and produced *Double Falshood, or The Distrest Lovers* (1728) as a 'revised and adapted' form of a play which he said was 'written originally' by Shakespeare. John Ozell (*d.* 1743) gave English versions of many French plays.

l. 290. *Heideggre.* John James Heidegger, of Swiss origin, was the manager of the opera-house in the Haymarket, and of the masquerades. He joked upon his own ugliness and was caricatured by Hogarth.

l. 296. *Withers*, George Wither (1588–1667), the poet, held in low esteem in Pope's day and Dryden's. *Ward.* See l. 233. *Gildon.* See *Epistle to Arbuthnot*, l. 151, and note.

l. 297. *high-born Howard*, Edward Howard (*fl.* 1670), author of the 'incomparable, incomprehensible poem' *The British Princes*: see *The Spectator*, No. 43.

l. 298. *Fool of Quality*, probably Lord Hervey. See *Epistle to Arbuthnot*, l. 305.

PAGE **98**, l. 309. *Archer's wing*, Thomas Archer, groom-porter to the king.

l. 321. *Familiar White's*. See l. 203 note.

l. 324. *pious Needham*, 'mother Needham', a notorious procuress.

l. 326. *Hockley-hole*. See above, l. 222 note.

l. 328. *Ogilby*. See l. 141 note.

l. 330. *God save King Log*. Pope says in a note that this hemistich is taken from Ogilby's version of the *Frogs and their King* in his translation of Aesop's *Fables*.

Book III

PAGE **99**, ll. 67–100. In this passage the goddess-mother shows the new king the progress of intellectual obscurantism through history, and the steady advance of ignorance and superstition in the Dark Ages. This passage deals with the past as the next illustrates the present and future.

l. 75. *One god-like Monarch*. 'Chi-Ho-am-ti, Emperor of China, the same who built the great wall between China and Tartary, destroyed all the books and learned men of that empire' (Pope's note).

l. 82. *their Physic of the Soul*. 'The Caliph, Omar I, having conquered Ægypt, caused his General to burn the Ptolomæan library, on the gates of which was this inscription, *ΨΥΧΗΣ ΙΑΤΡΕΙΟΝ*, the Physic of the Soul' (Pope's note).

ll. 87, 88. *Lo! where Mæotis sleeps*. Johnson was told that this was the couplet by which Pope declared his own ear to be most gratified (*Life of Pope, ad fin.*).

l. 96. *The soil that arts*. 'Phœnicia, Syria, &c. where Letters are said to have been invented. In these countries Mahomet began his conquests' (Pope's note).

PAGE **100**, ll. 317–40. The final coronation of the hero and a visionary glimpse of the glories of his reign, signalized by the promotion of the unworthy and inept and the neglect and sufferings of the witty and intelligent, together with the total collapse of cultural and scholarly traditions. The Fourth Book deals with the full and detailed accomplishment of this vision.

l. 324. *Our Midas*. Cibber was corrector of plays at Drury Lane Theatre.

l. 325. *Benson*, William (1682–1754), surveyor-general of

works. The monument to Milton which he erected in Westminster Abbey in 1737 bore his own name on it.

l. 326. *Ambrose Philips* was given official appointments in Ireland, under the patronage of Hugh Boulter, Archbishop of Armagh.

l. 327. *Ripley,* Thomas (*d.* 1758), architect. He built the Admiralty, Whitehall, 1724–6. *Jones* is Inigo Jones, whose banqueting-house in Whitehall 'had been for many years so neglected as to be in danger of ruin' (Pope). *Boyle* is Richard Boyle, third Earl of Burlington.

l. 329. *Wren,* Sir Christopher, was superseded by Benson as surveyor-general of works in 1718, and died in retirement, but not therefore 'in sorrow', in 1723.

l. 340. *Iv'ry Gate.* See *Aeneid,* vi. 893–6.

Book IV. The Conclusion

PAGES **101–2.** This passage, the most familiar in the whole *Dunciad,* ends this great progress of dulness and pedantry and intellectual pretentiousness in a final and abiding darkness of the mind. The anarchy, which man's will and wit had so long tried to dissolve, returns, and all collapses in one stupendous and meaningless chaos.

PAGE **101,** l. 608. G——, Dr. John Gilbert, Bishop of Llandaff; afterwards Bishop of Salisbury and Archbishop of York.

MORAL ESSAYS

The *Moral Essays* and *Essay on Man* are fragments of what was to have been a much longer poem. Spence quotes Pope as giving the following account of the plan (*Anecdotes,* p. 315): 'I had once thoughts of completing my ethic work in four books. —The first, you know, is on the Nature of Man.—The second, would have been on Knowledge and its limits:—here would have come in an Essay on Education; part of which I have inserted in the *Dunciad.*—The third, was to have treated of Government; both ecclesiastical and civil—and this was what chiefly stopped my going on. I could not have said what *I would* have said, without provoking every church on the face of the earth: and I did not care for living always in boiling water. —This part would come into my Brutus, which is all planned already; and even some of the most material speeches written in prose.—The fourth, would have been on Morality; in eight or nine of the most concerning branches of it: four of which would have been the two extremes to each of the Cardinal Virtues.'—

The only part of this project that Pope managed to complete

was the *Essay on Man*. The *Moral Essays* may have been designed originally as a part of the Fourth Book—that on morality.

THE DUKE OF BUCKINGHAM

PAGE **103.** George Villiers, second Duke of Buckingham (1625–87), Zimri in *Absalom and Achitophel*, was wit, courtier, statesman, and leader of Restoration society. A minor poet, he had the chief share in that very clever burlesque *The Rehearsal* (1671), which is largely devoted to ridiculing Dryden. Pope's account of his death is highly rhetorical and over-coloured, but it is a good example of his manner in this kind of writing. This duke was no relation to John Sheffield, Duke of Buckingham (1648–1721), Adriel in *Absalom and Achitophel*, who, as Lord Mulgrave, had befriended Dryden, and whose collected *Works* were edited by Pope in 1723. See *Epistle to Arbuthnot*, l. 139.

l. 9. *Cliveden*, Buckingham's stately house on the Thames.

l. 10. *wanton Shrewsbury*, Anna Maria, Countess of Shrewsbury, Buckingham's mistress, whose husband he killed in a duel.

THE FIRST SATIRE OF THE SECOND BOOK OF HORACE

This is the first official defence offered by Pope of his satiric method. He had recently been bitterly attacked for having satirized the Duke of Chandos as Timon in his *Epistle to Burlington* (1731), now known as the fourth of the *Moral Essays*.

PAGE **104.** *his Learned Council* was William Fortescue, at this time Attorney-General to the Prince of Wales. He became Master of the Rolls in 1741. He may have contributed to the *Memoirs of Scriblerus*.

l. 3. *wise Peter*, Peter Walter, a very rich attorney and usurer.

l. 4. *Chartres*, Francis Chartres, the most infamous of contemporary rakes.

l. 6. *Lord Fanny*, Lord Hervey; see *Epistle to Arbuthnot*, l. 305 note.

l. 8. *Council*, i.e. counsel.

l. 23. *Sir Richard*, Sir Richard Blackmore, the physician-poet. See *Epistle to Augustus*, l. 387 note.

PAGE **105,** l. 27. *Budgel*, Eustace Budgell (1686–1737), a cousin of Addison, wrote thirty-seven numbers of *The Spectator*. His latter years were unhappy, and, having incurred suspicion of forgery, discredited and heavily in debt, he drowned himself. See *Epistle to Arbuthnot*, ll. 378–9 note.

l. 30. *Carolina*, George II's queen.

l. 35. *Caesar scorns the Poet's lays.* Cf. *Epistle to Augustus,* l. 404.

l. 42. *A hundred smart in Timon and in Balaam.* For Timon, see *Moral Essay,* iv. 99 sqq.; for Balaam, *Moral Essay,* iii. 339 sqq. This is one of Pope's attempts to suggest that Timon's villa is not to be identified with Canons. See *Epistle to Arbuthnot,* ll. 299–300 note.

l. 46. *Darty,* Charles Dartineuf, a well-known *bon viveur* and wit.

l. 47. *Ridotta,* from *ridotto,* a rout or evening party; here used as a name for a type of Society woman.

l. 49. *Hockley-hole.* See *Dunciad,* i. 222 note.

l. 52. *downright Shippen.* William Shippen was the leader of the Jacobite group in the House of Commons. He was respected by all parties for his honesty.

PAGE **106,** l. 71. *Hectors,* a cant title for street-bullies.

l. 75. *Fleury,* Cardinal Fleury, chief minister of France. But in his last years (*ob.* 1743) France found herself involved in bitter and expensive wars.

l. 81. *Delia* has been identified with Lady Deloraine, whom gossip named a poisoner.

l. 82. *Page,* Sir Francis Page, a 'hanging' judge who tried Pope's protégé and Johnson's friend, Richard Savage, for murder. See Johnson's *Life of Savage.*

l. 83. *furious Sappho.* Lady Wortley Montagu saw here a reference to herself. Pope denied that she was Sappho in a letter of blazing sarcasm to Lord Peterborough.

l. 89. *Walters,* the Peter of l. 3.

PAGE **107,** l. 99. *Bedlam, or the Mint.* Cf. *Epistle to Arbuthnot,* l. 13.

l. 100. Nathaniel Lee had died insane and Budgell's debts were driving him to death.

l. 111. *Boileau,* see p. 13, l. 33 note.

PAGE **108,** l. 127. *St. John,* see p. 22, l. 27 note.

l. 129. *He,* Charles, Earl of Peterborough, the eccentric general who was one of the closest of Pope's aristocratic friends. Pope refers to Peterborough's extraordinary campaign of 1705–6.

AN ESSAY ON MAN

PAGE **109**. Pope had neither the temperament nor the knowledge for a big philosophical poem; his was certainly not a speculative mind. *An Essay on Man* reflects contemporary deist talk, and intellectually owes much to the doctrines of Leibniz. The suggestion that Pope merely versified what Bolingbroke wrote in prose has no sufficient foundation, but it is true that Bolingbroke's influence is everywhere visible. Although the intellectual content is thin, the poem is none the less a remarkable performance, Pope's technique enabling him to exploit to the full his tenuous philosophy. The least satisfactory of his major poems, it was nevertheless well received on its first appearance and contains passages that are beautiful as well as brilliant.

l. 1. *St. John*, see p. 22, l. 27 note.

l. 13. *shoot Folly as it flies*. Cf. Dryden and Tate, *Absalom and Achitophel*, Part 2, l. 1032; 'Observes, and shoots their Treasons as they fly'.

l. 16. *vindicate the ways of God to Man*. Cf. *Paradise Lost*, i. 26: 'Justify the ways of God to men'.

PAGE **110**, l. 29. *this frame*, the universe considered as an arranged system in accordance with Leibniz's theory of Pre-established Harmony.

l. 41. *argent*. Cf. *Paradise Lost*, iii. 460. 'Those argent fields.'

l. 42. *Jove's Satellites*. The four large satellites of Jupiter were discovered by Galileo, Jan. 7, 1610. The smaller ones remained unknown until the nineteenth century. Satellites has here the Latin pronunciation, i.e. four syllables.

l. 44. *Wisdom infinite*. Pope begins his argument by assuming this axiom from Leibniz, *Théodicée*, i. 8: 'Cette suprême sagesse, jointe à une bonté qui n'est pas moins infinie qu'elle n'a pu manquer de choisir le meilleur.' Optimism as defined by Leibniz does not mean that of all systems possible God has chosen absolutely the best, but the best as conducive to the end intended in the creation.

l. 47. *Then, in the scale of reas'ning life*. The theory of a scale of beings gradually descending from perfection to non-entity, and complete in every intermediate rank and degree, was developed by Leibniz. Pope's lines speak only of the extant species of organized beings. Leibniz's conception was much more extended, and regarded the whole of space and time as an unbroken chain of mutually related existences and occurrences.

PAGE **111**, l. 64. *Ægypt's God*, the sacred bull at Memphis, called Apis by the Greeks.

l. 88. *sparrow fall*. Cf. St. Matthew, x. 29.

AN EPISTLE TO ARBUTHNOT

PAGE **114**. John Arbuthnot (1667–1735), to whom Pope addressed this his most intimate and personal poem, was the sanest and most delightful of the Scriblerus group. Physician to Queen Anne and a strong Tory, he was at once a noted wit and a sound scholar, as is shown by his *Law is a Bottomless Pit, or, the*

History of John Bull (1712), and his *Tables of Ancient Coins, Weights and Measures* (1727). This *Epistle* was published in January 1735, two months before Arbuthnot died. On July 17, 1734, writing to Pope from Hampstead, he says: 'And I make it my last request, that you will continue that noble disdain and abhorrence of vice which you seem naturally endued with, but still with a due regard to your own safety; and study more to reform than chastise, though the one cannot be effected without the other.'

The following are extracts from Pope's letters to Arbuthnot dated respectively August 2, August 25, and September 3 in the same year: 'I thank you, dear Sir, for making that your request to me, which I make my pride, nay my duty;—"that I should continue my disdain and abhorrence of vice, and manifest it still in my writings". I would indeed do it with more restrictions, and less personally; it is more agreeable to my nature, which those who know it not are greatly mistaken in. But general satire in times of general vice has no force and is no punishment: people have ceased to be ashamed of it when so many are joined with them; and it is only by hunting one or two from the herd that any examples can be made. . . . I hope to deter, if not to reform.'

'I took very kindly your advice, concerning avoiding ill-will from writing Satire, and it has worked so much upon me (considering the *time* and *state* you gave it in), that I determine to address to you one of my Epistles, written by piecemeal many years, and which I have now made haste to put together; wherein the question is stated, what were, and are my motives of writing, the objections to them, and my answers. It pleases me much to take this occasion of testifying (to the public at least, if not to posterity), my obligation and friendship for and from you, for so many years; that is all that is in it; for compliments are fulsome and go for nothing.'

'. . . it has given me time to finish the Poem I told you of, which I hope may be the best Memorial I can leave, both of my friendship to you, and of my own character being such as you need not be ashamed of that friendship. The Apology is a bold one, but true: and it is truth and a clear conscience that I think will set me above all my enemies, and make no honest man repent of having been my friend.'

The *Epistle to Arbuthnot* is Pope's most ample *apologia* for his career and writings, for his satirical methods and for his moral and social ideals. A detailed study of it is essential to the understanding of his character: he reveals himself in it not only as the man he was, but, hardly less important, as the man he wished to be considered by his friends and known to posterity. It is the finest example in English poetry of the familiar style.

The poem was afterwards called by Warburton the 'Prologue to the Satires'.

PAGE **116,** l. 1. *good John.* John Searle, Pope's gardener. *A Plan of Mr. Pope's Garden,* by 'J. Serle, his Gardener', was published in 1745.

l. 8. *They pierce my thickets . . . glide.* The grounds of Pope's villa at Twickenham were cut in two by the road from London to Hampton Court. To avoid crossing this road he had an underground passage made beneath it which contained his famous grotto.

l. 13. *the Mint.* The district in Southwark which was in the neighbourhood of what had formerly been the Mint was a sanctuary for debtors. They were free from arrest on Sundays.

l. 20. *With desp'rate charcoal.* Cf. Martial, *Epigr.*, xii. 61.

l. 23. *Arthur.* Arthur Moore (1666–1730), Commissioner of Trade and Plantations under Queen Anne.

whose giddy son, James Moore or Moore Smythe, who is pilloried in *The Dunciad,* ii. 35–50.

PAGE **117,** l. 40. *nine years.* Horace, *Ars Poetica,* 388, 'Nonum prematur in annum.'

l. 49. *Pitholeon,* a 'foolish poet of Rhodes' mentioned by Horace, *Satires,* I, x. 22; the name is here given to Leonard Welsted.

l. 53. *Curl,* Edmund Curll (1683–1747), bookseller, who published pirated editions and scandalous books.

l. 62. *Lintot,* Bernard Lintot (1675–1736), who had been Pope's publisher from 1712 to 1726. They broke over the terms of the sale of the *Odyssey.*

PAGE **118,** l. 69. *Midas.* The story is told by Ovid, *Met.* xi. 174–93, of Midas's barber; and by Chaucer, in *The Wife of Bath's Tale,* of Midas's queen.

l. 85. *Codrus,* a name for a poetaster. See Juvenal, *Sat.* i. 2.

l. 86. *Thou unconcern'd canst hear,* a parody of Addison's version of Horace, *Odes,* III. iii. 14–16:

> 'Should the whole Frame of Nature round him break;
> In Ruin and Confusion hurl'd,
> He, Unconcern'd, would hear the mighty Crack.'

This last line was given by Pope, in *The Art of Sinking in Poetry,* as an instance of bathos due to 'one choice word that ends the line'.

PAGE **119,** l. 99. *Bavius,* a name for a wretched poet; see Virgil, *Eclogue,* iii. 90.

l. 100. *Still to one Bishop*. See note on Ambrose Philips, *Dunciad*, iii. 326.

l. 113. *This prints my letters*. In 1726 a collection of Pope's letters was published by Curll.

l. 117. *Ammon's great son*, Alexander the Great.

l. 122. *immortal Maro*, Virgil.

ll. 125 sqq. This passage of personal history, followed by a commemoration of his friends, recalls Ovid, *Tristia*, IV. x. 19 sqq. See note on p. 21, l. 23.

l. 130. *no father disobey'd*. Pope's father encouraged him in writing verses. He was difficult to satisfy and, when at last pleased, would say 'These be good rhymes'.

PAGE **120**, l. 135. *Granville the polite*, George Granville (1666–1735), created in 1711 Lord Lansdowne of Bideford. See note on p. 21, l. 10. He died on January 30, about a fortnight after the publication of the *Epistle to Arbuthnot*. Pope dedicated to him his *Windsor-Forest*.

l. 136. *knowing Walsh*. William Walsh (1663–1708) was one of the first to recognize Pope's merits. In the *Essay on Criticism*, l. 729, Pope calls him 'The Muse's judge and friend, Who justly knew to blame or to commend'. Dryden in 1697 called him 'the best critic of our nation'. He it was who advised Pope to aim at correctness.

l. 137. *Well-natur'd Garth*, Sir Samuel Garth, M.D. (1661–1719), highly distinguished as a physician, and the author of *The Dispensary* (1699).

l. 138. *Congreve*, William Congreve (1670–1729), the dramatist.

l. 139. *courtly Talbot*, Charles Talbot, twelfth Earl and first Duke of Shrewsbury (1660–1718), 'the King of Hearts', statesman, and dilettante.

Somers, John Somers, Baron Somers of Evesham (1651–1716), Lord Chancellor 1697. Swift dedicated to him the *Tale of a Tub*, and Addison the first volume of the collected edition of *The Spectator*.

Sheffield, John Sheffield, Duke of Buckingham: cf. p. 103, note.

l. 140. *mitred Rochester*, see note on *Atterbury*, p. 21, l. 23.

l. 141. *St. John's self*, see p. 22, l. 27 note.

great Dryden's friends before. Swift never forgave Dryden's sentence on his early poems, 'Cousin Swift you will never be a poet'. Disparity of age prevented any real friendship between Dryden and St. John.

l. 146. *Burnets, Oldmixons, and Cooks*. Thomas Burnet (1694–1753), son of Bishop Burnet who wrote the *History of My Own Time*, was in his young days a member of Addison's circle and had attacked Pope in *Homerides* (1715) and in *The Grumbler* (1715). Pope thought him—but wrongly—the author of *Pope Alexander's Supremacy and Infallibility Examin'd* (1729). He appears in *The Dunciad*, iii. 179–84. After a boisterous career he attained high and deserved honour as a Justice of the Court of Common Pleas, and was latterly on better terms with Pope. See *The Letters of Thomas Burnet to George Duckett*, ed. D. Nichol Smith, 1914.

John Oldmixon (1673–1742), Whig pamphleteer and historian. He attacked Pope in *The Arts of Logick and Rhetorick, illustrated* (1728). See *The Dunciad*, ii. 283.

Thomas Cooke (1703–56), commonly known as 'Hesiod Cooke' because of his translation of Hesiod, attacked Pope in *The Battle of the Poets* (1725). In a note to *The Dunciad*, ii. 138, Pope says that 'he also published some malevolent things in the British, London, and Daily Journals; and at the same time wrote letters to Mr. Pope protesting his innocence'.

l. 148. *pure Description*, as in the *Pastorals* and *Windsor-Forest*.

l. 150. Cf. Addison, *Letter from Italy* (1703), 183–4:

> 'My Humble verse requires a softer Theme,
> A painted meadow, or a purling Stream.'

ll. 151–214. An earlier version of these lines is printed in *Miscellanies* (1727), vol. iii, with the heading 'Fragment of a Satire'.

l. 151. *Gildon*, Charles Gildon (1665–1724) began the attack in *A New Rehearsal, or Bays the Younger* (1714), and continued it in his *Complete Art of Poetry* (1718). See note on ll. 193–214 below.

l. 153. *Dennis*, see p. 34, l. 270 note.

ll. 159 sqq. *Pains, reading, study*, &c. Pope, like Swift in *A Tale of a Tub*, despised the minute scholars who pursued learning for its own sake. The views here stated are given fuller expression in *The Dunciad*, iv. 189–238. Richard Bentley (1662–1742), the greatest classical scholar of the age, was in his eyes only a 'verbal critic'. Unfortunately Bentley's wild emendations in his edition of Milton's *Paradise Lost* (1732) gave real occasion for satire. *Tibalds*, i.e. Lewis Theobald (1688–1744), was a man of mean powers in comparison with Bentley, but his edition of Shakespeare (1733) was in many ways superior to Pope's (1725). In 1726 he brought out *Shakespeare restored: or, a Specimen of the Many Errors, as well Committed, as Unamended, by Mr. Pope*.

PAGE **121**, l. 179. *pilfer'd Pastorals*. The Pastorals of Ambrose

Philips—published along with Pope's Pastorals in Tonson's *Miscellany*, vi. 1709—were no further pilfered than that they contained the stock-in-trade of all pastoral writers. They were a professed imitation of Spenser, as Pope's were of Virgil. In 1709 Philips had translated from the French, for Tonson the publisher, *The Thousand and One Days: Persian Tales.*

l. 192. In the 'Fragment of a Satire' printed in 1727 this line reads 'How would they swear, not *Congreve's* self was safe!'

PAGES **121–2,** ll. 193–214. These celebrated lines are a masterpiece of Pope's skill in satirical portraiture. They first got into print, it would appear, in *The St. James's Journal,* Dec. 15, 1722, and were reprinted by Curll in *Cythereia* (1723), *Court Poems* (1726), and *Miscellanea* (1727). They were next printed in the third volume of Pope's and Swift's *Miscellanies,* published by B. Motte in 1727, before they were incorporated by Pope in this poem. But the first draft had been written at least as early as 1718, and had been sent by Pope to Addison himself (Spence, *Anecdotes,* pp. 148–9, and *Letters of Thomas Burnet,* 1914, ed. D. Nichol Smith, pp. xl–xli). The immediate provocation seems to have been a booklet entitled *Memoirs of the Life of William Wycherley, Esq. with a Character of his Writings. By the Right Honourable George Lord Lansdown,* which appeared in 1718. It should, however, be noted that Pope spoke of the satire as having been sent to Addison 'about three years' before Addison's death, which occurred in June 1719. The booklet was written by Gildon and published by Curll—Lansdowne had indeed written the *Character of the Writings,* the title-page making it appear that he was responsible for the whole book—and contained highly scurrilous and insulting references to Pope, who, early in his career, had been for a while intimate with Wycherley. The young Earl of Warwick, Addison's stepson, told Pope that Addison had paid Gildon ten guineas to write this 'thing about Wycherley', and Pope believed him. Hence perhaps l. 151 with its reference to Gildon's 'venal quill'. Pope had earlier resented Addison's avowed preference for Tickell's Translation of Homer to his own version, and originally had written after l. 208 the couplet (as printed in *Cythereia*):

> 'Who, when *Two Wits* on rival *Themes* contest,
> Approves of *Both,* but likes the *Worst* the *Best.*'

When finally revising these lines he omitted this direct reference to an old personal misunderstanding and changed the name 'Addison' to 'Atticus'. It should be remembered that Pope did appreciate Addison's 'true Genius': see especially *Epistle to Augustus,* ll. 215–20.

PAGE **121,** l. 198. *like the Turk.* Cf. John Denham, *On Fletcher's Works*, ll. 23–4:

'Eastern Kings, who to secure their reign,
Must have their Brothers, Sons, and Kindred slain.'

PAGE **122,** l. 211. *Templars*, members of the Inns of Court. *raise*, applaud.

l. 215. *rubric on the walls.* The titles of new books were printed in red letters as advertisements: cf. *The Dunciad*, i. 40.

l. 216. *claps*, bills clapped or stuck on a wall, posters; cf. French *affiche.*

l. 218. *On wings of winds*, &c., a verse of Hopkins's version of Psalm 104.

l. 222. *a birth-day song.* The Poet Laureate throughout the eighteenth century, and till the time of Southey, wrote a New Year's Ode and a Birth-day Ode every year. George II hated 'boets and bainters'.

l. 225. *daggled*, led or trailed about, through wet or mire.

PAGES **122–3,** ll. 230–48. Bufo has traditionally been supposed to be Charles Montagu, Earl of Halifax (1661–1715). The last four lines seem to refer to him, but the rest of the portrait is not more applicable to him than to any pretentious patron of poetry. In the Chauncy MS. of this *Epistle* the name is said to be not 'Bufo' but 'Bubo'—the name which Pope gave to Bubb Doddington: see l. 280 note. Perhaps Doddington gave the first suggestions for this character. In all probability Bufo was at first a separate character study, like Atticus; and in any case Pope's object in this *Epistle* was to represent the literary patron in general, and there was no reason why he should not reinforce what was originally suggested by one patron by what he knew of another. He is thinking more of the type than of the individual.

PAGE **123,** l. 236. *a true Pindar.* 'Ridicules the affectation of Antiquaries, who frequently exhibit the headless *Trunks* and *Terms* of Statues, for Plato, Homer, Pindar, &c.' (Pope's note).

l. 245. *what wonder?* Dryden had his patrons, but there was good reason why he should hold aloof from Halifax, who as a young man had joined with Prior in writing *The Hind and the Panther transvers'd* (1687), the most effective of the retorts to Dryden's poem *The Hind and the Panther.*

l. 248. *help'd to bury.* Halifax is said to have offered to pay the expenses of a private funeral for Dryden and to give £500 for a monument. See Johnson's *Life of Dryden.*

ll. 256–60. *Gay.* John Gay (1685–1732) lived latterly with the Duke and Duchess of Queensberry. The epitaph on his monument in Westminster Abbey was written by Pope.

l. 262. *To live and die,* borrowed from Sir John Denham, *Of Prudence*:

'Learn to live well, that thou may'st dye so too;
To live and dye is all we have to do.'

PAGE **124,** l. 280. *Sir Will,* Sir William Yonge, Secretary at War 1735–46, noted for his ready and fluent speech.

Bubo, George Bubb Doddington (1691–1772), created Lord Melcombe in 1761. The two are coupled again in the *Epilogue to the Satires,* i. 68:

'The Flow'rs of Bubo, and the Flow of Yonge.'

ll. 299–300. *the Dean . . . Cannons.* See *Moral Essays,* iv. 141–50:

'And now the Chapel's silver bell you hear,
That summons you to all the Pride of Pray'r . . .
To rest, the Cushion and soft Dean invite,
Who never mentions Hell to ears polite.'

These lines occur in the description of Timon's Villa, a satire on soulless magnificence. The description was suggested mainly by Canons, the great mansion of the first Duke of Chandos near Harrow (built 1712, demolished 1749), but Pope had introduced details that were not literally true of Canons, e.g. the 'silver bell' and the 'soft Dean'. Pope's satire was general in intention, but was taken to be a satire on Chandos in particular. This identification had done Pope harm, even among his friends, for Chandos had been kind to him. See Johnson's *Life of Pope* and Spence, *Anecdotes,* p. 145.

PAGE **125,** l. 305. *Sporus.* John, Lord Hervey (1696–1743), son of the Earl of Bristol, was personally attached to the Court of George II, in the capacity of vice-chamberlain. Pope had attacked him under the name of 'Lord Fanny', and Hervey replied in *Verses to the Imitator of Horace* and in an *Epistle from a Nobleman at Hampton Court to a Doctor of Divinity* (1733). The original Sporus was one of Nero's minions. This is the least generalized of all the characters in this Epistle and shows the strongest personal animus. See J. W. Croker's Introduction to Lord Hervey's *Memoirs* for an account of his feud with Pope.

l. 319. *at the ear of Eve, familiar Toad*: see Milton, *Paradise Lost,* iv. 800. Hervey was the confidential adviser of Queen Caroline.

PAGE **126,** l. 341. *stoop'd to Truth.* 'The term is from falconry; and the allusion to one of those untamed birds of spirit, which sometimes wantons at large in airy circles before it regards, or *stoops to,* its prey' (Warburton's note).

l. 349. *The blow unfelt.* A lampoon called *A Pop upon Pope* (1728) recounted how Pope had been whipped in Ham Walks and how he had shed tears.

l. 351. *Th' imputed trash*, 'Such as profane Psalms, Court-Poems, and other scandalous things, printed in his Name by Curll and others' (Pope's note).

l. 353. *the pictur'd shape*. Pope was only four feet six inches in height and hunch-backed, and he was sensitive to the numerous caricatures which emphasized his deformity.

l. 363. *Japhet*, Japhet Crook, alias Sir Peter Stranger, forger and swindler. Cf. *Epilogue to the Satires*, i. 120, 'Shall Japhet pocket, like his Grace, a Will'; and *Moral Essays*, iii. 86.

l. 365. *Knight of the post*, a man who sought employment as a hired witness.

PAGE **127**, l. 375. *Welsted's lye*. 'This Man had the Impudence to tell in print, that Mr. *P.* had occasion'd a *Lady's death*, and to *name* a person he never heard of. He also publish'd that he had libell'd the Duke of *Chandos*; with whom (it was added) that he had liv'd in familiarity, and received from him a Present of *five hundred pounds*: The Falsehood of which is known to his Grace, whom Mr. *P.* never had the honour to see but *twice*, and never receiv'd any Present farther than the Subscription for *Homer*, from him, or from Any Great Man whatsoever' (Pope's note).

Leonard Welsted (1688–1747), minor poet and translator of Longinus, wrote several attacks on Pope, and won his place in *The Dunciad*, ii. 207 and iii. 169.

l. 378. *charge low Grubstreet on his quill*, charge Pope's pen with contributions to *The Grub-street Journal*. Pope in a note says, with doubtful truth, that in this paper 'he never had the least hand, direction, or supervisal'.

l. 379. *except his Will*. Budgell was suspected of having forged a will of Matthew Tindal in his own favour. See *First Satire of the Second Book of Horace*, l. 27 note.

l. 380. *the two Curls*, Curll and Lord Hervey, who is here coupled with the libellous bookseller, as above, l. 363, with Japhet Crook.

l. 388. *Of gentle blood*. Pope claimed erroneously to be connected on his father's side with the Earls of Downe. His mother was daughter of William Turner, a Roman Catholic gentleman of Yorkshire. One of her brothers is said to have been killed, and another to have died, 'in the service of King Charles'.

l. 391. *Bestia*. This allusion is doubtful.

l. 393. *marrying Discord*. This is supposed to be an allusion to Addison, who married the widowed Countess of Warwick.

l. 397. *Nor dar'd an Oath*. As a Roman Catholic he declined to take the various oaths which were then necessary qualifications for civil offices.

PAGE **128**, ll. 406–13. When this *Epistle* was published Mrs.

Pope had been dead eighteen months. She died June 7, 1733. Pope's filial piety is well attested and the sentiments expressed in these lines are deep and genuine. A first draft of them had been included in a letter sent to Aaron Hill on Sept. 3, 1731.

l. 417. *serv'd a Queen.* Arbuthnot had been physician to Queen Anne.

The First Epistle of the Second Book of Horace, Imitated

Page **129.** This is the most brilliant of Pope's *Epistles*, as *To Dr. Arbuthnot* is the most delightful. Unlike the latter it has a Latin original which it follows most skilfully, turning Horace's genuine tributes to Caesar Augustus into ironic praise of George Augustus. Specially noteworthy is the political satire at the beginning and close of the poem and the literary criticism which occupies the bulk of it. It is Pope's most important body of criticism in verse, more detailed, more particular, and more experienced than the *Essay on Criticism.* Its political attitude reflects that of the Tories and 'patriotic' Whig opponents of Walpole and the Queen.

Page **130.** *To Augustus.* Augustus was one of George II's names. Lord Hervey *Memoirs*, i. 305: 'Not that there was any similitude between the two princes besides their names. George Augustus neither loved learning nor encouraged men of letters, nor were there any Mæcenases about him. There was another essential difference between the two Augustuses; as personal courage was the only quality necessary to form a great prince, which the one was suspected to want, so I fear it was the only one the other was ever thought to possess.' One must remember, however, King George's patronage of Handel.

ll. 1–6. These lines are elaborately ironical; the government was unwilling to support the claims of English merchants against the Spaniards by force of arms.

Page **131,** l. 16. Cf. Waller, *A Panegyric to My Lord Protector*, ll. 147–8:

> 'But living virtue, all achievements past,
> Meets envy still, to grapple with at last.'

l. 38. *Skelton*, John Skelton (?1460–1529), now recognized as a vigorous poet of real gifts. A new edition of his works had appeared in 1736, and Pope may have heard from his friend Spence of its reception at Oxford. The 'Heads of Houses' are probably heads of Oxford Colleges.

l. 40. *Christ's Kirk o' the Green*, a poem of unknown authorship, attributed both to James I and James V of Scotland. It was edited by Edmund Gibson, Anglo-Saxon scholar, afterwards

Bishop of London, in 1691, and included in James Watson's *Choice Collection of Scots Poems*, 1706, and Allan Ramsay's *Ever Green*, 1724. Ramsay had added two cantos, 1718.

l. 42. *the Devil*, the Devil Tavern, between Temple Bar and the Middle Temple Gate, Ben Jonson's favourite resort.

PAGE **132**, l. 62. *courtesy of England*, a term 'restricted in law to the single case of not disturbing the husband in the enjoyment, for his life, of his wife's estate after her death'.

l. 66. *Stowe*, John Stow (1525–1604), Elizabethan chronicler and antiquary, compiler of *Annales of England*, frequently augmented and reprinted.

l. 75. *Cowley*. Abraham Cowley (1618–67) was probably the best-known English poet of his time. His collected works published in folio in the year after his death went through many editions, but he fell out of favour as Dryden came into it. His epic *Davideis* was 'forgot'; his *Pindarique Odes* were not 'forgot' only in so far as the fashion which they set still continued. The 'language of his heart' is found in the simpler passages where Cowley forgets his wit and his conscious art and speaks from deep feeling or with a quiet sincerity.

PAGES **132–3**, ll. 79–88. These lines embody the current criticism of the Town.

PAGE **133**, l. 85. *Shadwell hasty, Wycherly was slow.* Cf. Rochester, *An Allusion to The 10th Satyr of the 1st Book of Horace*:

> 'Of all our Modern Wits, none seem to me
> Once to have toucht upon true Comedy,
> But hasty Shadwell, and slow Wicherley,' &c.

For Shadwell see note on *Dunciad*, i. 240. William Wycherley (?1640–1716) had been one of the earliest of Pope's literary friends.

l. 86. *Southern*, Thomas Southerne (1660–1746), whose best-known plays are *The Fatal Marriage* (1694) and *Oroonoko* (1696).

Rowe, Nicholas Rowe (1674–1718), author of *Tamerlane* (1702), *The Fair Penitent* (1703), and *Jane Shore* (1714). He was the chief tragic writer of the reign of Queen Anne. In 1709 he published the earliest of the eighteenth-century editions of Shakespeare, and in 1715 succeeded Tate as Poet Laureate.

l. 87. *These, only these*, &c. The omission of Otway, author of *Venice Preserved*, may seem curious, but this is not a careful catalogue; it represents a list made hurriedly in conversation. Otway comes in later, l. 277.

l. 88. *eldest Heywood*, John Heywood (?1497–?1580), the chief dramatic writer of the reign of Henry VIII, author of *The Four PP*.

l. 91. *Gammer Gurton's Needle*, 'a ryght pithy, pleasaunt, and merrie comedie' by 'Mr. S.' (probably William Stevenson), acted in Christ's College, Cambridge, and printed in 1575. It was reprinted in 1661.

l. 92. *the Careless Husband* (1704), by Colley Cibber; see *The Dunciad*, i. 32 note.

l. 98. *Sydney's verse.* Sir Philip Sidney (1554–86) experimented in his *Arcadia* with imitations of classical measures.

l. 104. *desp'rate Hook*, a jibe at Bentley's emendations in his edition of *Paradise Lost* (1732). See *Epistle to Arbuthnot*, ll. 159 sqq. note.

l. 109. *Sprat*, Thomas Sprat (1635–1713), Bishop of Rochester, whose best-known works are his *History of the Royal Society* (1667) and the *Life* of his friend Cowley (1668). Pope called him 'a worse Cowley' (Spence, *Anecdotes*, p. 173).

Carew, Thomas Carew (?1594–?1639), a lyric poet of real quality.

Sedley, Sir Charles Sedley (?1639–1701), poet and notable wit, author of the song beginning 'Not Celia, that I juster am'.

l. 110. *Miscellanies.* A favourite method of publishing poems was in collections containing pieces by various authors. Among the best known are the six volumes of Tonson's *Miscellanies*—with which Dryden's name is associated—1684 to 1709.

PAGE **134,** l. 122. *Betterton*, Thomas Betterton (1635–1710), the leading actor of Dryden's time.

l. 123. *Booth*, Barton Booth (1681–1733), who played the part of Cato in Addison's play (1713).

l. 142. Cf. Lansdowne's *The Progress of Beauty*, ll. 179, 180:

> 'From the loud Palace to the silent Grove,
> All by the King's Example live, and love.'

PAGE **135,** l. 153. *On each enervate string.* '*The Siege of Rhodes* by Sir William Davenant, the first opera sung in England' (Pope's note).

l. 182. *Ward.* 'A famous empiric, whose pill and drop had several surprising effects, and were one of the principal subjects of writing and conversation at this time' (Pope's note).

l. 183. *Radcliff's Doctors*, holders of the medical fellowships at University College, Oxford, founded by John Radcliffe (1650–1714), the most famous physician of his day. They had to spend part of their time 'in parts beyond sea for their better improvement'.

PAGE **136,** l. 186. *Ripley.* See *Dunciad*, p. 100, l. 327. He built Houghton for Sir Robert Walpole.

l. 214. *Roscommon*, Wentworth Dillon, Earl of Roscommon (1633–85), author of *An Essay on Translated verse*, 1684.

PAGES **136–7,** ll. 215–20. See note on *Epistle to Arbuthnot,* ll. 193–214.

PAGE **137,** ll. 221–8. A magnificent tribute to Swift. Cf. *The Dunciad,* i. 19–26 and note.

l. 226. *relieve the Idiot.* Cf. Swift's poem *On the Death of Dr. Swift* (1731),

'He gave the little wealth he had
To build a house for fools and mad.'

Swift also in his lifetime instituted a fund for granting small loans to artisans and tradesmen of good character.

PAGE **138,** l. 263. *We conquer'd France.* This passage represents Horace's 'Græcia capta, ferum victorem cepit', &c. (*Epis.* II. i. 156).

l. 267. *Waller was smooth.* See *Essay on Criticism,* l. 361 and note.

Dryden. The triplet with the last line an alexandrine is introduced more frequently by Dryden than by any other great master of the heroic couplet, and Pope uses it here to illustrate the qualities which he mentions. This is one of the few triplets in all the verse of Pope.

l. 279. *fluent Shakespear.* See the address '*To the great Variety of Readers*' prefixed by John Heminge and Henry Condell to the First Folio (1623), 'His mind and hand went together: And what he thought, he uttered with that easinesse, that wee have scarse received from him a blot in his papers'; and cf. Ben Jonson, *Discoveries,* 'I remember the Players have often mentioned it as an honour to Shakespeare, that in his writing, whatsoever he penned, he never blotted out a line. My answer hath been "Would he had blotted a thousand".'

PAGE **139,** l. 288. *Farqu'ar,* George Farquhar (1678–1707), author of *The Beaux' Stratagem* (1707).

l. 289. *Van,* Sir John Vanbrugh (1664–1726), author of *The Relapse* (1696) and *The Provoked Wife* (1697). He was the architect of Blenheim Palace and Castle Howard.

l. 290. *Astræa,* Mrs. Aphra Behn (1640–89), the first English professional authoress.

l. 292. *Cibber.* See *The Dunciad,* i. 32 note; *the laws* are the laws of conventional dramatic procedure.

l. 293. *poor Pinky,* William Pinkethman, comic actor and showman, mentioned frequently in *The Spectator.* Cf. *The Tatler,* No. 188: '*Penkethman* devours a cold chicken with great Applause.'

l. 309. *the Black-joke.* There was a popular indecent song called 'The Coal-black Joke'.

l. 313. *From heads to ears.* 'From *Plays* to *Operas*, and from *Operas* to *Pantomimes*' (Warburton's note).

l. 319. *Old Edward's Armour.* For the performance of the coronation scene in *Henry VIII* at the time of the coronation of George II, the armour of one of the kings of England had been borrowed from the Tower.

PAGE **140,** l. 328. *on Orcas' stormy steep.* 'The farthest Northern Promontory of Scotland, opposite to the Orcades' (Pope's note).

l. 331. *Quin,* James Quin (1693–1766), the leading actor before Garrick. The 'high plume' which he affected is seen in the engraving of 'Quin as Coriolanus' reproduced in Doran's *Annals of the English Stage.*

Oldfield, Anne Oldfield (1683–1730), the most famous actress of her time.

l. 338. *railly,* a common form in the seventeenth and eighteenth centuries: Fr. *railler.*

PAGE **141,** l. 355. *Merlin's Cave.* 'A building in the Royal Gardens of Richmond, where is a small but choice Collection of Books' (Pope's note). An ironical sneer at the literary taste of Queen Caroline, for whom the building was made.

l. 379. *Fit to bestow.* Walpole in 1730 had made Cibber Poet Laureate.

l. 381. *Bernini* (1598–1680), painter, sculptor, and architect. His bust of Charles I is not now known.

l. 382. *Kneller,* Sir Godfrey Kneller (1646–1723), whose painting of William III is now at Windsor.

l. 387. *One knighted Blackmore.* Sir Richard Blackmore (*d.* 1729) was knighted as court physician, not as poet.

Quarles. See *Dunciad,* i. 140 note. Quarles was a Royalist, but there is no evidence that Charles I pensioned him; nor is Jonson known to have spoken of him.

PAGE **142,** l. 389. *No Lord's anointed.* The allusion to the 'Russian Bear' awaits an explanation.

ll. 394–403. These lines are the most heavily charged with irony in the whole poem.

l. 410. *A vile Encomium.* Cf. Shaftesbury, *Advice to an Author,* Part II, Sect. i (ed. 1710, p. 73; *Characteristicks,* 1711, i, p. 226): 'Vile *Encomiums* and wretched *Panegyricks* are the worst of *Satyrs.*'

l. 413. *Praise undeserv'd is scandal in disguise,* a quotation from an anonymous poem 'The Celebrated Beauties' in Tonson's *Miscellany,* vi (1709), p. 514.

l. 417. *Eusden,* Lawrence Eusden (1688–1730), Cibber's predecessor as Poet Laureate.

Philips. See *Dunciad*, iii. 326, and *Epistle to Arbuthnot*, ll. 100 and 179.

Settle. See *Dunciad*, i. 90 note.

l. 419. *Bedlam*, Bethlehem Hospital.

Soho, Wardour Street, originally called Old Soho. Both these neighbourhoods were centres of the trade in old books.

One Thousand Seven Hundred and Thirty Eight

In 1742 Pope published the fourth book of *The Dunciad* and in 1743 he recast the whole of that poem. With these exceptions the two dialogues of *One Thousand Seven Hundred and Thirty Eight* are his last important poems. They were published in May and July 1738, the former appearing on the same day as Johnson's *London*, and are as fresh and vigorous as anything he ever wrote. The fragment of *Dialogue II* here printed offers a proud and triumphant plea for the employment of the terrors of satire in the public interest.

Page **143**, l. 9. *F.* stands for 'Friend'.

PRINTED IN GREAT BRITAIN
AT THE UNIVERSITY PRESS, OXFORD
BY VIVIAN RIDLER
PRINTER TO THE UNIVERSITY